How to access your on-line resources

Kaplan Financial students will have a MyKaplan account and these extra resources will be available to you online. You do not need to register again, as this process was completed when you enrolled. If you are having problems accessing online materials, please ask your course administrator.

If you are not studying with Kaplan and did not purchase your book via a Kaplan website, to unlock your extra online resources please go to **www.en-gage.co.uk** (even if you have set up an account and registered books previously). You will then need to enter the ISBN number (on the title page and back cover) and the unique pass key number contained in the scratch panel below to gain access.

You will also be required to enter additional information during this process to set up or confirm your account details.

If you purchased through the Kaplan Publishing website you will automatically receive an e-mail invitation to register your details and gain access to your content. If you do not receive the e-mail or book content, please contact Kaplan Publishing.

This code can only be used once for the registration of this book online. This registration and your online content will expire when the examinations covered by this book have taken place. Please allow one hour from the time you submit your book details for us to process your request.

Please scratch the film to access your unique code.

Please be aware that this code is case-sensitive and you will need to include the dashes within the passcode, but not when entering the ISBN.

CIMA's CGMA 2019 Professional Examinations

CIMA's CGMA Operational Level

Subject F1

Financial Reporting

EXAM PRACTICE KIT

British Library Cataloguing-in-Publication Data

A catalogue record for this book is available from the British Library.

Published by:

Kaplan Publishing UK
Unit 2 The Business Centre
Molly Millar's Lane
Wokingham
Berkshire
RG41 2QZ

ISBN: 978-1-83996-472-5

© Kaplan Financial Limited, 2023

The text in this material and any others made available by any Kaplan Group company does not amount to advice on a particular matter and should not be taken as such. No reliance should be placed on the content as the basis for any investment or other decision or in connection with any advice given to third parties. Please consult your appropriate professional adviser as necessary. Kaplan Publishing Limited, all other Kaplan group companies, the International Accounting Standards Board, and the IFRS Foundation expressly disclaim all liability to any person in respect of any losses or other claims, whether direct, indirect, incidental, consequential or otherwise arising in relation to the use of such materials. Printed and bound in Great Britain.

Kaplan Publishing's learning materials are designed to help students succeed in their examinations. In certain circumstances, CIMA can make post-exam adjustment to a student's mark or grade to reflect adverse circumstances which may have disadvantaged a student's ability to take an exam or demonstrate their normal level of attainment (see CIMA's Special Consideration policy). However, it should be noted that students will not be eligible for special consideration by CIMA if preparation for or performance in a CIMA CGMA© exam is affected by any failure by their tuition provider to prepare them properly for the exam for any reason including, but not limited to, staff shortages, building work or a lack of facilities etc.

Similarly, CIMA will not accept applications for special consideration on any of the following grounds:

- failure by a tuition provider to cover the whole syllabus
- failure by the student to cover the whole syllabus, for instance as a result of joining a course part way through
- failure by the student to prepare adequately for the exam, or to use the correct pre-seen material
- errors in the Kaplan Official Study Text, including sample (practice) questions or any other Kaplan content or
- errors in any other study materials (from any other tuition provider or publisher).

Acknowledgements

This product contains copyright material and trademarks of the IFRS Foundation®. All rights reserved. Used under licence from the IFRS Foundation®. Reproduction and use rights are strictly limited. For more information about the IFRS Foundation and rights to use its material please visit www.ifrs.org.

Disclaimer: To the extent permitted by applicable law the Board and the IFRS Foundation expressly disclaims all liability howsoever arising from this publication or any translation thereof whether in contract, tort or otherwise (including, but not limited to, liability for any negligent act or omission) to any person in respect of any claims or losses of any nature including direct, indirect, incidental or consequential loss, punitive damages, penalties or costs.

Information contained in this publication does not constitute advice and should not be substituted for the services of an appropriately qualified professional.

IFRS

The IFRS Foundation logo, the IASB logo, the IFRS for SMEs logo, the 'Hexagon Device', 'IFRS Foundation', 'eIFRS', 'IAS', 'IASB', 'IFRS for SMEs', 'IASs', 'IFRS', 'IFRSs', 'International Accounting Standards' and 'International Financial Reporting Standards', 'IFRIC', NIIF® and 'SIC' are **Trade Marks** of the IFRS Foundation.

IFRS

Trade Marks

The Foundation has trade marks registered around the world (**'Trade Marks'**) including 'IAS®', 'IASB®', 'IFRIC®', 'IFRS®', the IFRS® logo, 'IFRS for SMEs®', IFRS for SMEs® logo, the 'Hexagon Device', 'International Financial Reporting Standards®', NIIF® and 'SIC®'.

Further details of the Foundation's Trade Marks are available from the Licensor on request.

CONTENTS

	Page
Index to questions and answers	P.7
Exam techniques	P.9
Syllabus guidance, learning objectives and verbs	P.11
Approach to revision	P.15
Syllabus grids	P.17

Section

1	Objective test questions	1
2	Answers to objective test questions	75
3	References	119

This document references IFRS® Standards and IAS® Standards, which are authored by the International Accounting Standards Board (the Board), and published in the 2022 IFRS Standards Red Book.

Quality and accuracy are of the utmost importance to us so if you spot an error in any of our products, please send an email to mykaplanreporting@kaplan.com with full details.

Our Quality Co-ordinator will work with our technical team to verify the error and take action to ensure it is corrected in future editions.

INDEX TO QUESTIONS AND ANSWERS

OBJECTIVE TEST QUESTIONS

	Page number	
	Question	Answer
Principles of tax (Questions 1 to 91)	1	75
The Regulatory Environment of Financial Reporting (Questions 92 to 139)	24	88
Financial statements (Questions 140 to 205)	37	93
Managing cash and working capital (Questions 206 to 253)	60	109

EXAM TECHNIQUES

COMPUTER-BASED ASSESSMENT

Golden rules

1. Make sure you have completed the compulsory 15-minute tutorial before you start the test. This tutorial is available through the AICPA & CIMA website and focusses on the functionality of the exam. You cannot speak to the invigilator once you have started.

2. These exam practice kits give you plenty of exam style questions to practise so make sure you use them to fully prepare.

3. Attempt all questions, there is no negative marking.

4. Double check your answer before you put in the final answer although you can change your response as many times as you like.

5. Not all questions will be multiple choice questions (MCQs) – you may have to fill in missing words or figures.

6. Identify the easy questions first and get some points on the board to build up your confidence.

7. Attempt 'wordy' questions first as these may be quicker than the computation style questions. This will relieve some of the time pressure you will be under during the exam.

8. If you don't know the answer, flag the question and attempt it later. In your final review before the end of the exam try a process of elimination.

9. Work out your answer on the whiteboard provided first if it is easier for you. There is also an onscreen 'scratch pad' on which you can make notes. You are not allowed to take pens, pencils, rulers, pencil cases, phones, paper or notes into the testing room.

SYLLABUS GUIDANCE, LEARNING OBJECTIVES AND VERBS

A   CIMA's CGMA® 2019 PROFESSIONAL QUALIFICATION

Details regarding the content of CIMA's CGMA 2019 Professional Qualification can be located within the CGMA 2019 Professional Qualification syllabus document.

You can use the following diagram showing the whole structure of your qualification to help you keep track of your progress. Make sure you seek appropriate advice if you are unsure about your progression through the qualification.

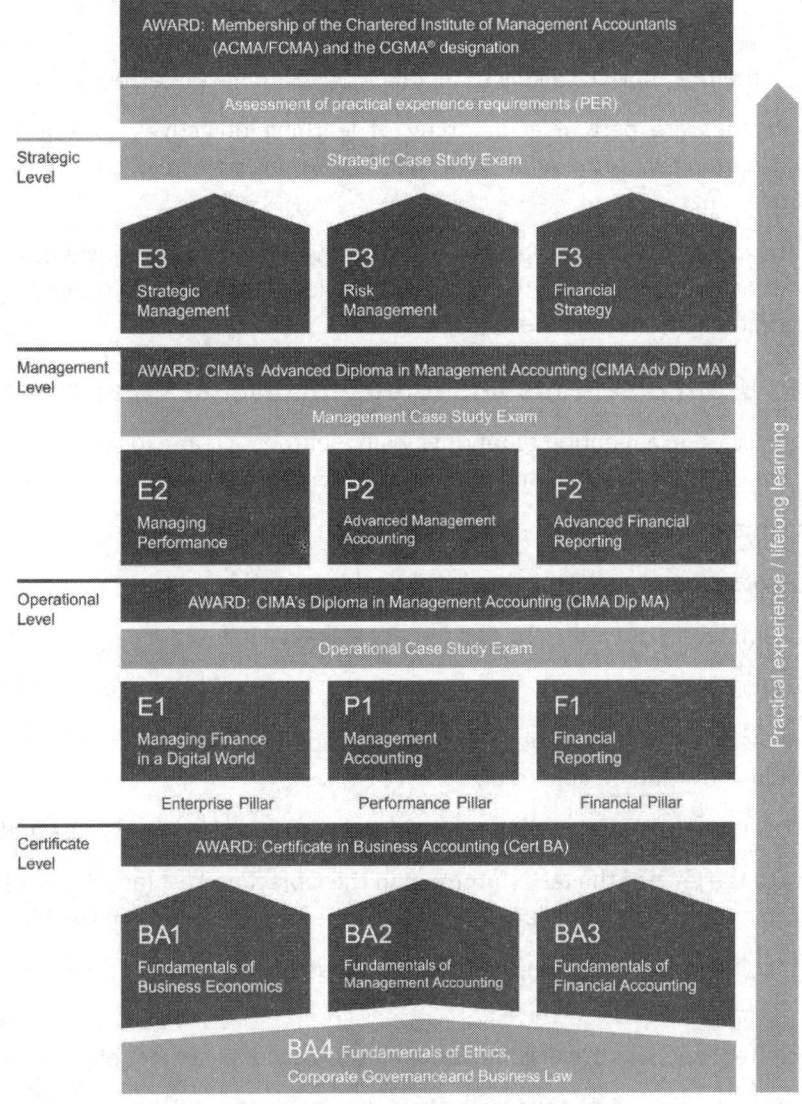

Reproduced with CIMA's permission

SUBJECT F1: FINANCIAL REPORTING

B STUDY WEIGHTINGS

A percentage weighting is shown against each exam content area in CIMA's CGMA® Exam Blueprints. This is intended as a guide to the proportion of study time each topic requires.

All component learning outcomes will be tested.

The weightings do not specify the number of marks that will be allocated to topics in the examination.

C LEARNING OUTCOMES

Each subject within the qualification is divided into a number of broad syllabus topics. The topics contain one or more lead learning outcomes, related component learning outcomes and indicative knowledge content.

A learning outcome has two main purposes:

1 to define the skill or ability that a well-prepared candidate should be able to exhibit in the examination

2 to demonstrate the approach likely to be taken by examiners in examination questions.

The learning outcomes are part of a hierarchy of learning objectives. The verbs used at the beginning of each learning outcome relate to a specific learning objective, e.g., Evaluate alternative approaches to budgeting.

The verb 'evaluate' indicates a high-level learning objective. As learning objectives are hierarchical, it is expected that at this level students will have knowledge of different budgeting systems and methodologies and be able to apply them.

CIMA's CGMA Exam Blueprints and representative task statements

CIMA has also published examination blueprints giving learners clear expectations regarding what is expected of them. This can be accessed via the AICPA & CIMA website.

The blueprint is structured as follows:

- Exam content sections (reflecting the syllabus document)
- Lead and component outcomes (reflecting the syllabus document)
- Representative task statements.

A representative task statement is a plain English description of what a CGMA® qualified finance professional should know and be able to do.

The content and skill level determine the language and verbs used in the representative task.

CIMA will test up to the level of the task statement in the Objective Test (an Objective Test question on a particular topic could be set at a lower level than the task statement in the blueprint).

The format of the Objective Test blueprints follows that of the published syllabus for the 2019 Professional Qualification.

Weightings for content sections are also included in the individual subject blueprints.

A list of the learning objectives and the verbs that appear in the syllabus learning outcomes and examinations follows and these will help you to understand the depth and breadth required for a topic and the skill level the topic relates to.

CIMA's verb hierarchy

Skill level	Verbs used	Definition
Level 5 **Evaluation** How you are expected to use your learning to evaluate, make decisions or recommendations	Advise	Counsel, inform or notify
	Assess	Evaluate or estimate the nature, ability or quality of
	Evaluate	Appraise or assess the value of
	Recommend	Propose a course of action
	Review	Assess and evaluate in order, to change if necessary
Level 4 **Analysis** How you are expected to analyse the detail of what you have learned	Align	Arrange in an orderly way
	Analyse	Examine in detail the structure of
	Communicate	Share or exchange information
	Compare and contrast	Show the similarities and/or differences between
	Develop	Grow and expand a concept
	Discuss	Examine in detail by argument
	Examine	Inspect thoroughly
	Interpret	Translate into intelligible or familiar terms
	Monitor	Observe and check the progress of
	Prioritise	Place in order of priority or sequence for action
	Produce	Create or bring into existence
Level 3 **Application** How you are expected to apply your knowledge	Apply	Put to practical use
	Calculate	Ascertain or reckon mathematically
	Conduct	Organise and carry out
	Demonstrate	Prove with certainty or exhibit by practical means
	Prepare	Make or get ready for use
	Reconcile	Make or prove consistent/compatible
Level 2 **Comprehension** What you are expected to understand	Describe	Communicate the key features of
	Distinguish	Highlight the differences between
	Explain	Make clear or intelligible/state the meaning or purpose of
	Identify	Recognise, establish or select after consideration
	Illustrate	Use an example to describe or explain something
Level 1 **Knowledge** What you are expected to know	List	Make a list of
	State	Express, fully or clearly, the details/facts of
	Define	Give the exact meaning of
	Outline	Give a summary of

D OBJECTIVE TEST

Objective Test

Objective Test questions require you to choose or provide a response to a question whose correct answer is predetermined.

The most common types of Objective Test question you will see are:

- Multiple choice, where you have to choose the correct answer(s) from a list of possible answers. This could either be numbers or text.
- Multiple response, for example, choosing two correct answers from a list of eight possible answers. This could either be numbers or text.
- Fill in the blank, where you fill in your answer within the provided space.
- Drag and drop, for example, matching a technical term with the correct definition.
- Hot spots, where you select an answer by clicking on graphs/diagrams.

Guidance on CIMA's on-screen calculator

As part of the CGMA Objective Test software, candidates are now provided with a calculator. This calculator is on-screen and is available for the duration of the assessment. The calculator is available in each of the Objective Tests and is accessed by clicking the calculator button in the top left hand corner of the screen at any time during the assessment. Candidates are permitted to utilise personal calculators as long as they are an approved CIMA model. CIMA approved model list can be found on the AICPA & CIMA website.

All candidates must complete a 15-minute exam tutorial before the assessment begins and will have the opportunity to familiarise themselves with the calculator and practise using it. The exam tutorial is also available online via the AICPA & CIMA website. Candidates can use their own calculators providing it is included in CIMA's authorised calculator listing.

Fundamentals of Objective Tests

The Objective Tests are 90-minute assessments comprising 60 compulsory questions, with one or more parts. There will be no choice and all questions should be attempted. All elements of a question must be answered correctly for the question to be marked correctly. All questions are equally weighted.

APPROACH TO REVISION

Stage 1: Assess areas of strengths and weaknesses

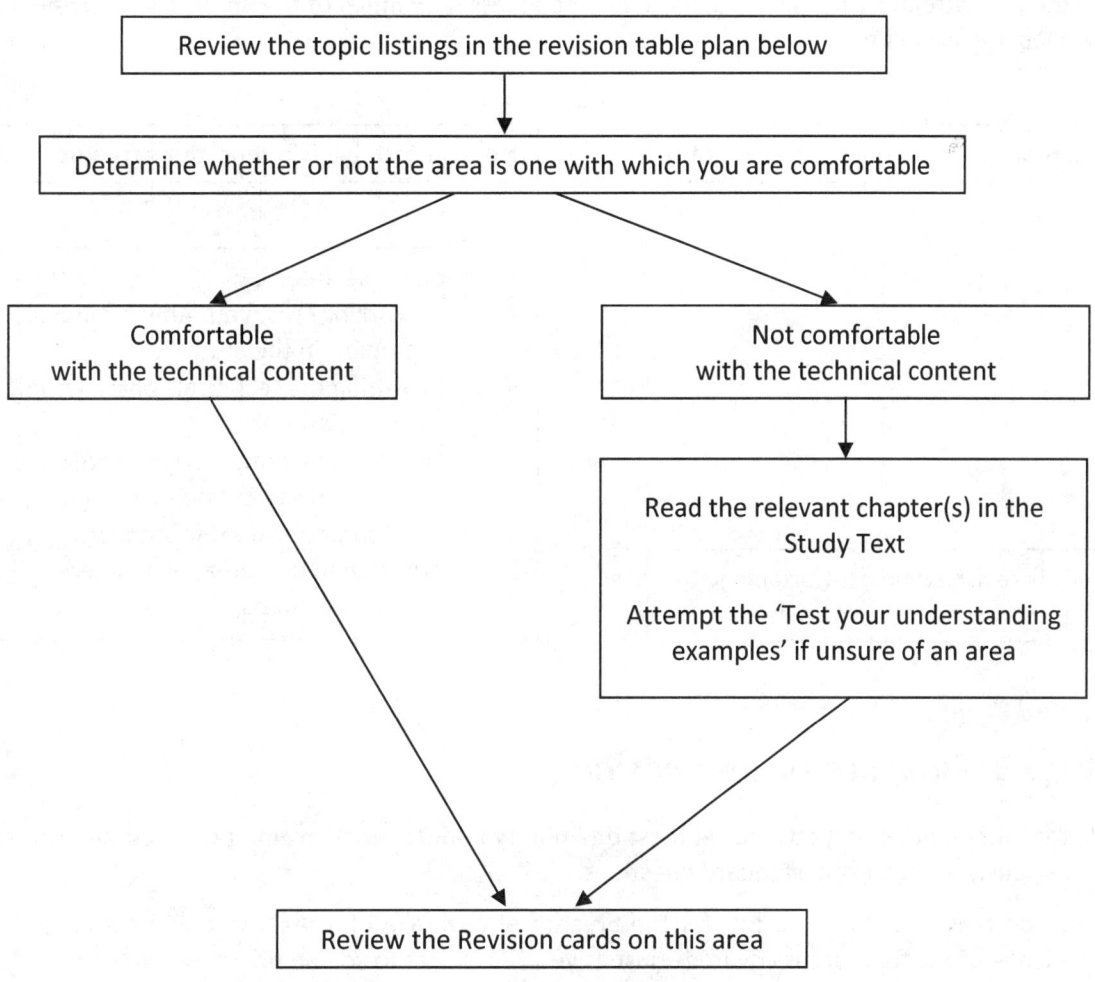

SUBJECT F1: FINANCIAL REPORTING

Stage 2: Question practice

Follow the order of revision of topics as recommended in the revision table plan below and attempt the questions in the order suggested.

Try to avoid referring to textbooks and notes and the model answer until you have completed your attempt.

Try to answer the question in the allotted time.

Review your attempt with the model answer and assess how much of the answer you achieved in the allocated exam time.

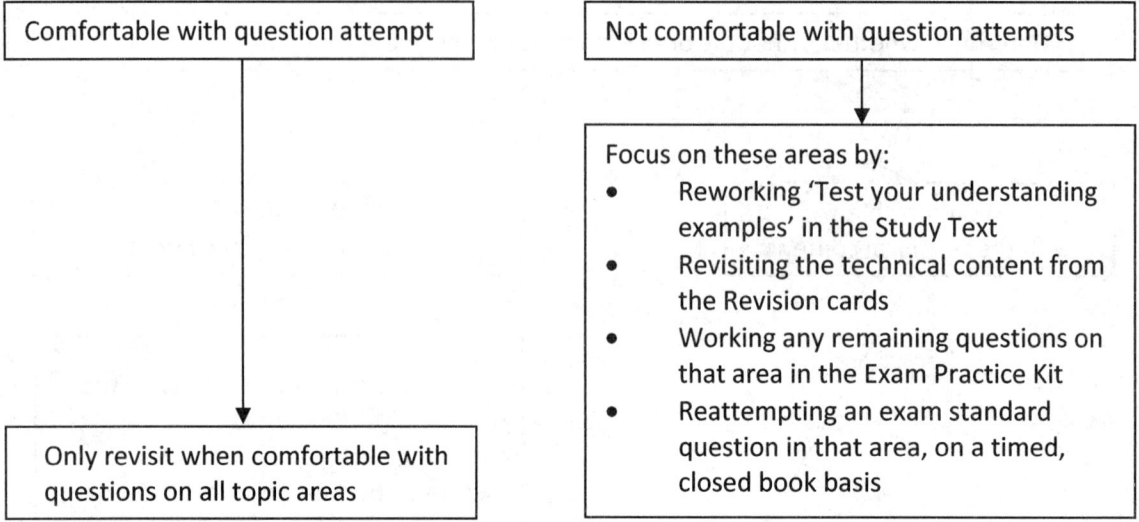

Stage 3: Final pre-exam revision

We recommend that you **attempt at least one ninety minute mock examination** containing a set of previously unseen exam standard questions.

It is important that you get a feel for the breadth of coverage of a real exam without advanced knowledge of the topic areas covered – just as you will expect to see on the real exam day.

Ideally a mock examination offered by your tuition provider should be sat in timed, closed book, real exam conditions.

SYLLABUS GRIDS

F1: Financial Reporting

What the finance function does and its implications

Content weighting

Content area		Weighting
A	Regulatory environment of financial reporting	10%
B	Financial statements	45%
C	Principles of taxation	20%
D	Managing cash and working capital	25%
		100%

SUBJECT F1: FINANCIAL REPORTING

F1A: Regulatory environment of financial reporting

The preparation of financial statements is regulated by laws, standards, generally accepted accounting principles and by codes. The regulations ensure that financial statements of different entities are comparable and that they present a reasonably accurate picture of the performance, position and prospects of the organisation to their users. This section covers who the regulators are, what they do and why and how the regulations are applied. The objective is to provide candidates with a strong foundation for preparing and interpreting financial statements.

Lead outcome	Component outcome	Topics to be covered	Explanatory notes
1 Identify regulators and describe their role.	a. Identify the major regulators. b. Describe what they do. c. Explain why they regulate financial reporting.	• National regulators • IFRS foundation • IASB • International Organisation for Securities Commissions (IOSCO) • Standard setting process • Differences between rules-based and principles-based regulations • Others such as International Integrated Reporting Council (IIRC)	Who are the regulators who determine how financial statements are prepared? What do they do? What value do they contribute to the production of financial statements? Coverage will include national and international regulators, stock exchange regulators and various accounting and financial reporting standards boards and major influential bodies like the IIRC.
2. Apply corporate governance principles to financial reporting.	a. Describe the role of the board in corporate governance. b. Apply corporate governance and financial stewardship principles to financial reporting.	• Need and scope for corporate governance regulations • Different approaches to corporate governance regulations	Boards have overall responsibility for ensuring that executives of organisations create value for their stakeholders and safeguard their assets. The role of boards is incorporated in various corporate governance codes. What are the main principles as they apply to financial reporting and the oversight of boards?

F1B: Financial statements

One of the roles of finance is to narrate how organisations create and preserve value. The financial statements are the means by which narration is done to particular audiences. This section enables candidates to prepare basic financial statements using financial reporting standards. It covers the main elements of the financial statements, what they intend to convey, the key financial reporting standards and how they are applied to prepare financial statements.

Lead outcome	Component outcome	Topics to be covered	Explanatory notes
1. Identify the main elements of financial statements.	a. Identify the main elements of financial statements contained in the IFRS conceptual framework.	• Objectives and overall purpose of financial reporting • Qualitative characteristics of financial information • Reporting entity and its boundaries • Recognition (and derecognition) • Measurement bases • Presentation and disclosure • Concept of capital maintenance	This sets the main principles that underpin the preparation of financial statements. The focus is on the main principles. No detailed treatments are expected.
2. Explain specific financial reporting standards.	Explain the specific financial reporting standards related to: a. Non-current assets b. Leases c. Impairment d. Inventory e. Events after the period	• IAS 16 – Property, Plant & Equipment • IFRS 5 – Non-current Assets Held for Sale or Discontinued Operations • IFRS 16 – Leases • IAS 36 – Impairment of Assets • IAS 2 – Inventories • IAS 10 – Events After the Reporting Period	Examine the requirements for how major items of the financial statements are to be recognised, measured and disclosed. This covers the main areas and not specialist topics.
3. Apply financial reporting standards to prepare basic financial statements.	Apply financial reporting standards to prepare: a. Statement of financial position b. Statement of comprehensive income c. Statement of changes in equity d. Statement of cash flows	IAS 1 – Presentation of Financial Statements IAS 7 – Statement of Cash Flows	Give hands-on experience of preparing basic financial statements by bringing in all the elements.

SUBJECT F1: FINANCIAL REPORTING

F1C: Principles of taxation

One of the implications of value creation is how that value is distributed to different stakeholders. Taxation is part of this distribution. This section helps candidates distinguish between types of taxes and to calculate corporate taxes. In a digital world where revenue is earned through online trading that spans national boundaries, candidates are introduced to the issues relating to taxation across international borders and the ethics of taxation.

Lead outcome	Component outcome	Topics to be covered	Explanatory notes
1. Distinguish between different types of taxes.	Distinguish between a. Direct versus indirect b. Corporate versus personal	• Features of direct and indirect taxes • Features of corporate and personal taxes	Gives a broad overview of the different types of taxes, who they affect and why they are used.
2. Calculate tax for corporates.	a. Explain the basis of taxation b. Explain the difference between accounting profit and taxable profit c. Calculate corporate tax	• Exempt income • Income taxed under different rules • Allowable expenditure • Capital allowances • Reliefs • Tax on sale of asset	The focus shifts here to corporate taxation. The main area covered is the difference between accounting profit and profit for taxation purposes. No national law is applied here. The main thing here is coverage and application of principles.
3. Explain some relevant issues that affect taxation.	Explain: a. Taxation across international borders b. Ethics of taxation	• Corporate residence • Types of overseas operations (e.g., subsidiary or branch) • Double taxation • Transfer pricing • Tax avoidance • Tax evasion	Given the increase of cross-border trading and revenue generation in the digital world what are the key issues affecting international taxation? What are the ethical issues that arise in the computation and payment of taxes?

F1C: Principles of taxation

F1D: Managing cash and working capital

Cash is the life blood of any organisation. The ability to provide cash, at the appropriate cost when it is needed is one of the key contributions that finance makes to organisations. It fulfils finance's role of enabling organisations to create and preserve value. This section provides candidates with the tools to ensure that the organisation has enough cash to ensure its continuing operations.

Lead outcome	Component outcome	Topics to be covered	Explanatory notes
1. Distinguish between the types and sources of short-term finance.	Distinguish between a. Types of short-term finance b. Financial institutions	• Trade payables • Overdrafts • Short-term loans • Debt factoring • Trade terms • Trade partners • Banks	What are the main types of funds needed for the short term? Where can those funds be accessed? How does one determine which type or source of finance is appropriate?
2. Explain and calculate operating and cash cycles.	Explain and calculate a. Operating cycle b. Cash flow cycle	• Inventory days • Trade receivable days • Trade payable days	The operating and cash cycle is one of the main means of putting together various elements of cash and near-cash items in a coherent manner to explain the cash needs of the organisation. What are these elements? How do they affect the availability and adequacy of cash for short-term operations?
3. Apply different techniques used to manage working capital.	a. Apply policies relating to elements of operating and cash cycle b. Prepare forecasts c. Explain risks relating to working capital	• Receivables management • Payables management • Inventory management • Risk of overtrading • Short-term cash flow forecasting • Investing short-term cash	What are the policies that organisations should put in place to manage working capital? How is the appropriate level determined, forecasted and accessed? What are the risks associated with accessing such funds?

Information concerning formulae and tables will be provided via the AICPA & CIMA website www.aicpa-cima.com.

Section 1

OBJECTIVE TEST QUESTIONS

PRINCIPLES OF TAX

1   Complete the sentence below by placing one of the following options in the space.

    Competent jurisdiction is _____.

    | the country whose tax laws apply to the entity |
    | the country the income arises in |
    | the country where the parent is incorporated |

2   Complete the sentence below by placing one of the following options in the space.

    A taxable person is _____.

    | the person or entity who is responsible for completing the tax return |
    | the person or entity who is accountable for the tax payment |
    | the person or entity who has direct contact with the tax authority |

3   Which TWO of the following are methods used for double tax relief?

    A   Exemption relief

    B   Deduction relief

    C   Tax loss relief

    D   Withholding relief

    E   Underlying relief

4   Which of the following could be said to be a progressive tax?

    A   Property sales tax of 1% of the selling price of all properties sold

    B   Value added tax at a rate of 0%, 10% or 15% depending on the type of goods or services provided

    C   Corporate wealth tax at 2% of total net assets up to $10 million then at 0.5% on net assets greater than $10 million

    D   Personal income tax of 10% on earnings up to $10,000, then at 15% from $10,001 up to $100,000 and 25% over $100,000

SUBJECT F1: FINANCIAL REPORTING

5 Complete the sentence below by placing one of the following options in the space.

Tax evasion is _____.

| a legal way of avoiding paying taxes |
| an illegal way of avoiding paying taxes |

6 An ideal tax system should conform to certain principles. Which of the following statements is NOT generally regarded as a principle of an ideal tax?

- A It should be fair to different individuals and should reflect a person's ability to pay
- B It should not be arbitrary, it should be certain
- C It should raise as much money as possible for the government
- D It should be convenient in terms of timing and payment

7 Complete the sentence below by placing one of the following options in the space.

A direct tax is one that _____.

| is passed onto another part of the economy |
| is imposed on the final consumer |
| is levied directly on the person who is intended to pay the tax |

8 Which of the following statements is NOT a source of tax rules in a country?

- A Domestic legislation
- B Directives from a supranational body
- C International treaties
- D International accounting standards

9 Which of the following incidence is being described here "This is the person who has direct contact with the tax authorities, i.e. who is legally obliged to pay the tax."

- A Formal incidence
- B Actual incidence
- C Partial incidence
- D Legal incidence

10 Which of the following is NOT a benefit of pay-as-you-earn (PAYE) method of tax collection?

- A It makes payment of tax easier for the tax payer as it is in instalments
- B It makes it easier for governments to forecast tax revenues
- C It benefits the tax payer as it reduces the tax payable
- D It improves government's cash flow as cash is received earlier

OBJECTIVE TEST QUESTIONS : SECTION 1

11 Which of the following is NOT a reason for governments to set deadlines for filing tax returns and payment of taxes?

    A   To enable governments to enforce penalties for late payments

    B   To ensure tax deducted at source by employers is paid over promptly

    C   To ensure tax payers know when they have to make payment

    D   To ensure that the correct amount of tax revenue is paid

12 Which of the following powers is a tax authority least likely to have granted to them?

    A   Power of arrest

    B   Power to examine records

    C   Power of entry and search

    D   Power to give information to other countries' tax authorities

13 The OECD model tax convention defines a permanent establishment to include a number of different types of establishments.

Which TWO of the following are included in the OECD's list of permanent establishments?

    A   A place of management

    B   A warehouse

    C   A subsidiary

    D   A quarry

    E   A building site that was used for nine months

14 In Country Y, A earns $75,000 profit for the year and receives a tax bill for $17,000.

B earns $44,000 profit for the year and receives a tax bill for $4,800.

Country Y's income tax could be said to be a:

    A   Regressive tax

    B   Proportional tax

    C   Progressive tax

    D   Fixed rate tax

15 Which THREE of the following statements are the main reasons why governments set deadlines for filing returns and/or paying taxes?

    A   The tax authority is more likely to get paid on time

    B   The payment will be more accurate

    C   The costs to collect the tax will be less

    D   The tax administration will be easier

    E   The tax authorities can forecast their cash flows

    F   They can impose penalties for late payment/late filing

SUBJECT F1: FINANCIAL REPORTING

16 In 1776, Adam Smith proposed that an acceptable tax should meet four characteristics. Three of these characteristics were certainty, convenience and efficiency.

Identify the FOURTH characteristic.

A   Neutrality

B   Transparency

C   Equity

D   Simplicity

17 Country X uses a Pay-As-You-Earn (PAYE) system for collecting taxes from employees. Each employer is provided with information about each employee's tax position and tables showing the amount of tax to deduct each period. Employers are required to deduct tax from employees and pay it to the revenue authorities on a monthly basis.

From the perspective of the government, which THREE of the following statements are the main advantages of the PAYE system?

A   Tax is collected regularly throughout the year so easier to forecast spending

B   The administrative costs are largely passed to the employers

C   Tax calculations are more accurate than the self-assessment system

D   The administrative costs are largely passed to the employees

E   Tax is collected regularly throughout the year so easier than making a large payment

F   There is less risk of default as tax is deducted at source

18 Place the THREE of the following options into the highlighted boxes in the table below to correctly reflect the characteristics of a commodity that, from a revenue authority's point of view, would make that commodity suitable for an excise duty to be imposed.

There are few large producers/suppliers
Demand is elastic with no close substitutes
Sales volumes are large
Demand is inelastic with no close substitutes
Sales volumes are small
There are many large producers/suppliers

Suitable for excise duties

OBJECTIVE TEST QUESTIONS : SECTION 1

19 Tax deducted at source by employers from employees' earnings and paid to government, often called pay-as-you-earn (PAYE) has a number of advantages.

Which TWO of the following are NOT likely to be seen as an advantage of PAYE by the government?

- (i) Most of the administration costs are borne by the employer.
- (ii) Employers may delay payment or fail to pay over PAYE deducted from employees.
- (iii) Employers may be inefficient and not deduct any tax or deduct the wrong amount from employees.
- (iv) Government receives a higher proportion of the tax due as defaults and late payments are fewer.

20 What is Hypothecation?

- A Process of earmarking tax revenues for specific types of expenditure
- B Estimation of tax revenue made by the tax authorities for budget purposes
- C Refund made by tax authorities for tax paid in other countries
- D Payment of taxes due to tax authorities, net of tax refunds due from tax authorities

21 The tax gap is the difference between:

- A when a tax payment is due and the date it is actually paid
- B the tax due calculated by the entity and the tax demanded by the tax authority
- C the amount of tax due to be paid and the amount actually collected
- D the date when the entity was notified by the tax authority of the tax due and the date the tax should be paid

22 Developed countries generally use three tax bases. One tax base widely used is income.

What are the other TWO widely used tax bases?

- A Assets
- B Profit
- C Consumption
- D Salary
- E Earnings

23 Which TWO of the following are most likely to encourage an increase in incidence of tax avoidance or tax evasion?

- (i) High penalties for tax evasion.
- (ii) Imprecise and vague tax laws.
- (iii) A tax system that is seen as fair to everyone.
- (iv) Very high tax rates.

SUBJECT F1: FINANCIAL REPORTING

24 Which of the following is NOT an advantage for the tax authority of deduction of tax at source?

    A   The total amount of tax due for the period is easier to calculate

    B   Tax is collected earlier

    C   Administration costs are borne by the entity deducting tax

    D   Tax is deducted before income is paid to the taxpayer

25 HD sells office stationery and adds a sales tax to the selling price of all products sold. A customer who purchases goods from HD has to pay the cost of the goods plus the sales tax. HD pays the sales tax collected to the tax authorities.

    From the perspective of HD the sales tax would be said to have:

    A   formal incidence

    B   effective incidence

    C   informal incidence

    D   ineffective incidence

26 Which of the following defines the meaning of tax gap?

    A   The difference between the tax an entity expects to pay and the amount notified by the tax authority

    B   The difference between the total amount of tax due to be paid and the amount actually collected by the tax authority

    C   The difference between the due date for tax payment and the date it is actually paid

    D   The difference between the amount of tax provided in the financial statements and the amount actually paid

27 Which of the following would be considered to be an example of an indirect tax?

    A   An entity assessed for corporate income tax on its profit

    B   An individual purchases goods in a shop, the price includes VAT

    C   An employee has tax deducted from salary through the PAYE system

    D   An individual pays capital gains tax on a gain arising on the disposal of an investment

28 Country Z has the following tax regulations in force for the years 20X5 and 20X6 (each year January to December):

- Corporate income is taxed at the following rates:
    - $1 to $10,000 at 0%
    - $10,001 to $25,000 at 15%
    - $25,001 and over at 25%.
- When calculating corporate income tax, Country Z does **not** allow the following types of expenses to be charged against taxable income:
    - entertaining expenses
    - taxes paid to other public bodies
    - accounting depreciation of non-current assets.
- Tax relief on capital expenditure is available at the following rates:
    - buildings at 4% per annum on straight line basis
    - all other non-current tangible assets are allowed tax depreciation at 27% per annum on reducing balance basis.

DB commenced business on 1 January 20X5 when all assets were purchased. No first year allowances were available for 20X5.

Non-current assets cost at 1 January 20X5

	$
Land	27,000
Buildings	70,000
Plant and equipment	80,000

On 1 January 20X6, DB purchased another machine for $20,000. This machine qualified for a first year tax allowance of 50%.

DB's Statement of profit or loss for the year to 31 December 20X6

	$
Gross profit	160,000
Administrative expenses	(81,000)
Entertaining	(600)
Tax paid to local government	(950)
Depreciation on buildings	(1,600)
Depreciation on plant and equipment	(20,000)
Distribution costs	(20,000)
	35,850
Finance cost	(1,900)
Profit before tax	33,950

Calculate DB's corporate income tax due for the year to 31 December 20X6.

$ _____. (Your answer should be rounded down to the nearest $.)

SUBJECT F1: FINANCIAL REPORTING

29 CFP, an entity resident in Country X, had an accounting profit for the year ended 31 December 20X1 of $860,000. The accounting profit was after charging depreciation of $42,000 and amortisation of development costs of $15,000 which should be treated as disallowable expenses.

CFP was entitled to a tax depreciation allowance of $51,000 for the year to 31 December 20X1.

Tax is charged at 25%.

CFP's tax payable for the year ended 31 December 20X1 is:

A $202,250

B $206,500

C $212,750

D $216,500

30 Which of the following defines the meaning of hypothecation?

A   A new tax law has to be passed each year to allow taxes to be legally collected

B   The difference between the total amount of tax due to be paid and the amount actually collected by the tax authority

C   Tax is deducted from amounts due before they are paid to the recipient

D   The products of certain taxes are devoted to specific types of public expenditure

31 Which of the following would NOT normally be considered a principle of a modern tax system?

A   Efficiency

B   Equity

C   Economic impact

D   Raise revenues

32 Complete the sentence below by placing one of the following options in the space.

Under the OECD model tax convention an entity will generally have residence for tax purposes in _____.

| the country of effective management |
| the country of incorporation |
| the country where most revenue is generated |

33 An entity earns a profit of $60,000 for the year to 31 March 20X2. The entity is assessed and owes $15,000 tax for the year.

Which of the following types of tax would best describe the tax due?

A   Capital tax

B   Income tax

C   Wealth tax

D   Consumption tax

34 Place the TWO of the following options into the highlighted boxes in the table below to correctly reflect TWO possible powers that a tax authority may be granted to enable it to enforce tax regulations.

| Power to review and query filed returns |
| Power to arrest |
| Power to enforce changes |
| Power to remove directors |
| Power to exchange information with tax authorities in other jurisdictions |

Powers of the tax authority

35 Which TWO of the following taxes commonly used by many countries would normally be defined as direct taxation

(i) import duty payable on specific types of imported goods

(ii) individual income tax, usually deducted at source

(iii) corporate income tax

(iv) value added tax.

36 Complete the sentence below by placing one of the following options in the space.

An example of an indirect tax would be _____.

| Excise duties |
| Trading income |
| Capital tax |

37 Tax authorities use various methods to reduce tax avoidance and tax evasion. **Which TWO of the above methods could be used to help reduce tax evasion and avoidance?**

(i) Increase tax rates to compensate for losses due to evasion.

(ii) Make the tax structure as complicated as possible.

(iii) Increase the perceived risk by auditing tax returns.

(iv) Simplify the tax structure, minimising allowances and exemptions.

38 Complete the sentence below by placing one of the following options in the space.

Tax avoidance is _____.

| a legal way of avoiding paying taxes |
| an illegal way of avoiding paying taxes |

SUBJECT F1: FINANCIAL REPORTING

39 Accounting depreciation is usually disallowed when calculating tax due by an entity and a deduction for tax depreciation is given instead.

Which of the following statements explains the reason why accounting depreciation is replaced with tax depreciation in a tax computation?

A Tax depreciation gives the tax payer more relief than accounting depreciation

B Tax depreciation gives the tax payer less relief than accounting depreciation

C To ensure that all entities are allowed the same rates of depreciation for tax purposes

D To ensure that the tax authority raises as much tax as possible

40 A customer purchases goods for $115, inclusive of VAT. From the customer's point of view the VAT could be said to be:

A a direct tax with formal incidence

B an indirect tax with formal incidence

C a direct tax with effective incidence

D an indirect tax with effective incidence

41 Country X has the following tax regulations in force:

- The tax year is 1 May to 30 April.
- All corporate profits are taxed at 20%.
- When calculating corporate taxable income, depreciation of non-current assets cannot be charged against taxable income.
- Tax depreciation is allowed at the following rates:
    - buildings at 5% per annum on straight line basis
    - all other non-current tangible assets are allowed tax depreciation at 25% per annum on a reducing balance basis.

No tax allowances are allowed on land or furniture and fittings.

FB commenced trading on 1 May 20X5 when it purchased all its non-current assets.

FB's non-current asset balances were:

	Cost 1 May 20X5 $	Carrying value 1 May 20X7 $	Tax written down value 1 May 20X7 $
Land	20,000	20,000	–
Buildings	80,000	73,600	72,000
Plant and equipment	21,000	1,000	11,812
Furniture and fittings	15,000	5,000	–

FB did not purchase any non-current assets between 1 May 20X5 and 30 April 20X7. On 2 May 20X7, FB disposed of all its plant and equipment for $5,000 and purchased new plant and equipment for $30,000. The new plant and equipment qualified for a first year tax allowance of 50%.

FB's Statement of profit or loss for the year ended 30 April 20X8

	$
Gross profit	210,000
Administrative expenses	(114,000)
Gain on disposal of plant and equipment	4,000
Depreciation – furniture and fittings	(5,000)
Depreciation – buildings	(3,200)
Depreciation – plant and equipment	(6,000)
Distribution costs	(49,000)
	36,800
Finance cost	(7,000)
Profit before tax	29,800

Calculate FB's corporate income tax due for the year ended 30 April 20X8.

$ _____. (Your answer should be rounded down to the nearest $.)

42 Governments use a range of specific excise duties as well as general sales taxes on goods.

Which of following don NOT explain a reason why a government might apply a specific excise duty to a category of goods?

- A   It may want to raise extra revenue from luxury products that people will buy regardless of cost
- B   To discourage use of harmful substances by making them expensive to buy, i.e. tobacco and alcohol
- C   To pay for the healthcare that harmful substances cause, i.e. medical treatment from smokers
- D   It may want to raise extra revenue from elastic products

43 Place the following options into the highlighted boxes in the table below to correctly show the difference between a single stage and a multi-stage sales tax. The options cannot be used more than once.

Tax at one level of production
This could be VAT
This could be cascade tax
Tax at each level of production
Single stage
Multi-stage

Type of tax		
Characteristic		
Characteristic		
Characteristic		

SUBJECT F1: FINANCIAL REPORTING

44 Once registered for VAT an entity must abide by the VAT regulations.

Which THREE of the following are typical requirements of VAT regulations?

A   Complete a quarterly VAT return

B   Charge VAT on all supplies to customers

C   Keep appropriate VAT records

D   Make payments to VAT authority and be able to claim back VAT when due

E   Recover VAT on all purchases from suppliers

F   Complete a monthly VAT return

45 Trading losses in any period can be carried back and set off against profits in the previous 12-month period, and any unrelieved losses should be carried forward to set against profits in future years. Trading losses cannot be set off against capital gains. Capital losses should be set off against capital gains in the same tax year, but unrelieved capital losses cannot be carried back. Unrelieved capital losses should be carried forward and set against capital gains in future years.

QWE had the following taxable profits, gains and losses in years 1 to 4.

	Trading profits/(losses) $	Capital gains/(losses) $
Year 1	50,000	6,000
Year 2	(90,000)	(8,000)
Year 3	30,000	5,000
Year 4	70,000	6,000

Place the following options into the highlighted boxes in the table below to correctly reflect QWE's taxable profits and gains in each year. The options can be used more than once and not all options have to be used.

$ nil
$3,000
$6,000
$10,000
$60,000

Year	Taxable profits	Taxable gains
1		
2		
3		
4		

46 What is the nature of group loss relief?

   A   Profits and losses of all companies in the same group are consolidated and taxed at the same rate

   B   Losses of subsidiaries must be set off against the profits of the parent company in the group

   C   Members of the group may surrender their losses to any other member of the group

   D   Companies in the same group are required by the tax authorities to surrender their losses to any other subsidiary in the group

47 Country B has a corporate income tax system that treats capital gains/losses separately from trading profits/losses. Capital gains/losses cannot be offset against trading profits/losses. All losses can be carried forward indefinitely, but cannot be carried back to previous years. Trading profits and capital gains are both taxed at 20%.

   BD had no brought forward losses on 1 October 20X2. BD's results for 20X3 to 20X5 were as follows:

	Trading profit/(loss) $000	Capital gains/(loss) $000
Year to September 20X3	200	(100)
Year to September 20X4	(120)	0
Year to September 20X5	150	130

   Place the following options into the highlighted boxes in the table below to correctly reflect BD's corporate income tax and capital tax due for each of the years ended 30 September 20X3 to 20X5. The options can be used more than once and not all options have to be used.

$ nil	$6,000
$14,000	$30,000
$16,000	$70,000
$40,000	$80,000

Year	Corporate income tax due	Capital tax due
30 September 20X3		
30 September 20X4		
30 September 20X5		

48 Which TWO of the following statements are reasons why a group of entities might want to claim group loss relief rather than use the loss in the entity to which it relates?

   A   Relief can be claimed as earlier because the surrendering entity does not expect to make a profit in the foreseeable future

   B   Tax can be saved because the entity the loss is surrendered to pays a lower rate of tax than the surrendering entity

   C   The surrendering entity will receive a tax refund for their loss if it is surrendered to another group entity

   D   Tax can be saved because the entity the loss is surrendered to pays a higher rate of tax than the surrendering entity

   E   The entity receiving the loss will receive a tax refund for the loss

SUBJECT F1: FINANCIAL REPORTING

49 BCF purchased an asset for $600,000 on 1 September 20X4. BCF incurred additional purchase costs of $5,000.

Indexation of the cost of BCF's asset is allowed in Country X. The relevant index increased by 60% in the period from 1 September 20X4 to 31 August 20Y1.

BCF sold the asset on 1 September 20Y1 for $1,200,000. BCF incurred selling costs of $9,000.

Assume all purchase and selling costs are tax allowable.

Tax is charged at 25%.

How much tax was due from BCF on disposal of its asset?

- A $55,750
- B $56,500
- C $64,250
- D $146,500

50 EG purchased a property for $630,000 on 1 September 20X0. EG incurred additional costs for the purchase of $3,500 surveyors' fees and $6,500 legal fees. EG then spent $100,000 renovating the property prior to letting it. All of EG's expenditure was classified as capital expenditure according to the local tax regulations.

Indexation of the purchase and renovation costs is allowed on EE's property. The index increased by 50% between September 20X0 and October 20X7. Assume that acquisition and renovation costs were incurred in September 20X0. EG sold the property on 1 October 20X7 for $1,250,000, incurring tax allowable costs on disposal of $2,000.

Calculate EG's tax due on disposal assuming a tax rate of 30%.

$ _____ . (Your answer should be rounded down to the nearest $.)

51 CG purchased an asset on 1 April 20X6 for $650,000, exclusive of import duties of $25,000. CG is resident in Country X where the indexation factor increased by 50% in the period from 1 April 20X6 to 31 March 20Y3.

CG sold the asset on 31 March 20Y3 for $1,200,000 incurring transaction charges of $17,000.

Capital gains are taxed at 25%.

Calculate the capital gains tax due from CG on disposal of the asset.

$ _____ . (Your answer should be rounded down to the nearest $.)

52 RS purchased an asset on 1 April 20X0 for $375,000, incurring legal fees of $12,000. RS is resident in Country X. There was no indexation allowed on the asset.

RS sold the asset on 31 March 20X3 for $450,000 incurring transaction charges of $15,000.

Tax is charged at 25%.

Calculate the capital gains tax due from RS on disposal of the asset.

$ _____ . (Your answer should be rounded down to the nearest $.)

OBJECTIVE TEST QUESTIONS : SECTION 1

53 The OECD Model tax convention defines a permanent establishment.

Which of the following is NOT specifically listed as a permanent establishment by the OECD Model tax convention?

- A   An office
- B   A factory
- C   An oil well
- D   A site of an 11 month construction project

54 Where a resident entity runs an overseas operation as a branch of the entity, certain tax implications arise.

Which of the following does NOT usually apply in relation to an overseas branch?

- A   Assets can be transferred to the branch without triggering a capital gain
- B   Corporate income tax is paid on profits remitted by the branch
- C   Tax depreciation can be claimed on any qualifying assets used in the trade of the branch
- D   Losses sustained by the branch are immediately deductible against the resident entity's income

55 A withholding tax is:

- A   tax withheld from payment to the tax authorities
- B   tax paid less an amount withheld from payment
- C   tax deducted at source before payment of interest or dividends
- D   tax paid on increases in value of investment holdings

56 Place the following options into the highlighted boxes in the table below to correctly show the difference between cascade sales tax and value added tax (VAT). The options can be used more than once and not all options have to be used.

| No refunds are provided by local government on purchase tax |
| Refunds are provided on purchase tax provided the purchases are used for a taxable supply |
| Tax at one level of production |
| Tax at each level of production |
| Single stage |
| Multi-stage |

Type of tax	Cascade tax	VAT
Characteristic		
Characteristic		
Characteristic		

SUBJECT F1: FINANCIAL REPORTING

57 JK, an entity operating in Country X, purchased land on 1 March 20X6 for $850,000. JK incurred purchase costs of surveyor's fees $5,000 and legal fees $8,000. JK spent $15,000 clearing the land and making it suitable for development. Local tax regulations classified all of JK's expenditure as capital expenditure.

JK sold the land for $1,000,000 on 1 February 20X9, incurring tax allowable costs of $6,000.

Tax is charged at a rate of 25%.

No indexation is allowable on the sale of land.

Calculate the capital tax payable by JK on the disposal of the land.

$ _____. (Your answer should be rounded down to the nearest $.)

58 **Complete the sentence below by placing one of the following options in the space.**

The Organisation of Economic Co-operation and Development's (OECD) model tax convention defines corporate residence.

Under the OECD model an entity will have residence in _____.

| the country of incorporation |
| the country where the directors reside |
| the country of effective management |
| the country where most production arises |

59 Corporate residence for tax purposes can be determined in a number of ways, depending on the country concerned.

Which of the following is NOT normally used to determine corporate residence for tax purposes?

A   The country from which control of the entity is exercised

B   The country of incorporation of the entity

C   The country where the management of the entity holds its meetings

D   The country where most of the entity's products are sold

60 The following details relate to EA:

- it was incorporated in Country A
- it carries out its main business activities in Country B
- its senior management operate from Country C and effective control is exercised from Country C.

Assume countries A, B and C have all signed double tax treaties with each other, based on the OECD model tax convention.

In which country will EA be deemed to be resident for tax purposes?

A   Country A

B   Country B

C   Country C

D   Both Countries B and C

61 EB has an investment of 25% of the equity shares in XY, an entity resident in a foreign country.

EB receives a dividend of $90,000 from XY, the amount being after the deduction of tax amounting to $10,000 deducted at source in the foreign country.

The $10,000 can be explained as what type of tax?

A Corporate tax

B Underlying tax

C Capital tax

D Withholding tax

62 Double tax relief is used to:

A ensure that you do not pay tax twice on any of your income

B mitigate taxing overseas income twice

C avoid taxing dividends received from subsidiaries in the same country twice

D provide relief where a company pays tax at double the normal rate

63 The following details are relevant:

- HC carries out its main business activities in Country A
- HC is incorporated in Country B
- HC's senior management exercise control from Country C, but there are no sales or purchases made in Country C
- HC raises its finance and is quoted on the stock exchange in Country D

Assume Countries A, B, C and D have all signed double taxation treaties with each other, based on the OECD model tax convention.

Which country will HC be deemed to be resident in for tax purposes?

A Country A

B Country B

C Country C

D Country D

64 AB made a profit of $320,000 for the year ended 31 December 20X2 and paid $80,000 tax on its profits. AB pays a gross dividend of $150,000 to its holding company, which operates in a foreign country. When AB pays the dividend it deducts a 10% tax.

This 10% tax is called:

A underlying tax

B corporate income tax

C foreign tax

D withholding tax

SUBJECT F1: FINANCIAL REPORTING

65 Which TWO of the following are methods of giving double taxation relief?

- A Tax credit relief
- B Deduction relief
- C Tax loss relief
- D Withholding relief
- E Underlying relief

66 Which of the following gives the meaning of rollover relief?

- A Trading losses can be carried forward to future years
- B Inventory can be valued using current values instead of original cost
- C Capital losses made in a period can be carried forward to future years
- D Payment of tax on a capital gain can be delayed if the full proceeds from the sale of an asset are reinvested in a replacement asset

67 Place the following options into the highlighted boxes in the table below to correctly the difference between exempt and zero rated supplies. The options cannot be used more than once.

| Entity must register for VAT purposes |
| Entity does not register for VAT purposes |
| VAT can be claimed back on purchases |
| VAT cannot be claimed back on purchases |

Type of supply	Zero rated	Exempt
Characteristic		
Characteristic		

68 Complete the sentence below by placing one of the following options in the space.

A capital gain is _____.

| the trading profit of an entity transferred to equity |
| the profit made on the disposal of a chargeable asset |
| the taxable profit of an entity |

69 Complete the sentence below by placing one of the following options in the space.

Capital tax is _____.

| the tax charged on the trading profit of an entity before it is transferred to equity |
| the tax charged on the profit made on the disposal of a chargeable asset |
| the tax charged on the taxable profit of an entity |

OBJECTIVE TEST QUESTIONS : SECTION 1

70 Complete the sentence below by placing one of the following options in the space.

A tax base represents _____.

| the tax written down value of an asset |
| what is being taxed |
| the taxable profit of an entity |

71 The tax year runs from 1 May to 30 April. An individual's accounting year ends on 31 December. AB's taxable profits for the year to 31 December 20X4 were $75,000.

The rate of tax chargeable on AB's profits is as follows:

Year to 30 April 20X4   20%
Year to 30 April 20X5   25%

On the basis of this information, calculate the tax payable for the year to 31 December 20X4.

$_____. (Your answer should be rounded down to the nearest $.)

72 Which THREE of following are examples of the different tax bases regularly used by governments?

- A Income
- B Equity
- C Capital
- D Benefits
- E Consumption
- F Losses

73 EF has an accounting profit before tax of $95,000. The tax rate on trading profits applicable to EF for the year is 25%. The accounting profit included non-taxable income from government grants of $15,000 and non-tax allowable expenditure of $10,000 on entertaining expenses.

Calculate the tax payable by EF for the year.

$_____. (Your answer should be rounded down to the nearest $.)

74 Complete the sentence below by placing one of the following options in the space.

Benefits in kind represent _____.

| all benefits given to an employee as part of their remuneration package |
| cash benefits given to an employee as part of their remuneration package |
| non-cash benefits given to an employee as part of their remuneration package |

SUBJECT F1: FINANCIAL REPORTING

75 For the year ended 30 September 20X2 KQ's income statement included a profit before tax of $147,000. KQ's expenses included political donations of $9,000 and entertaining expenses of $6,000.

KQ's statement of financial position at 30 September 20X2 included plant and machinery with a carrying value of $168,500. This is comprised of plant purchased on 1 October 20X0 at a cost of $180,000 and machinery purchased on 1 October 20X1 at a cost of $50,000.

KQ depreciates all plant and machinery on the straight line basis at 15% per year.

All expenses other than depreciation, amortisation, entertaining, taxes paid to other public bodies and donations to political parties are tax deductible.

Tax depreciation is deductible as follows:

- 50% of additions to property, plant and equipment in the accounting period in which they are recorded
- 25% per year of the written-down value (i.e. cost minus previous allowances) in subsequent accounting periods except that in which the asset is disposed of.

The corporate tax on profits is at a rate of 25%.

Calculate the tax payable by KQ for the year to 30 September 20X2.

$ _____. (Your answer should be rounded down to the nearest $.)

76 Which THREE of the following statements are true regarding excise duties?

    A   Suitable for inelastic products

    B   They are a unit tax

    C   Suitable for elastic products

    D   Suitable when there are few producers

    E   They are an ad valorem tax

    F   Suitable when there are many producers

77 EE reported accounting profits of $822,000 for the period ended 30 November 20X7. This was after deducting entertaining expenses of $32,000 and a donation to a political party of $50,000, both of which are disallowable for tax purposes.

EE's reported profit also included $103,000 government grant income that was exempt from taxation. EE paid dividends of $240,000 in the period.

Assume the tax rate is 25%.

Calculate EE's tax payable be on its profits for the year to 30 November 20X7.

$ _____. (Your answer should be rounded down to the nearest $.)

78 Place the following options into the highlighted boxes in the table below to correctly the difference between tax avoidance and tax evasion. The options cannot be used more than once.

| An illegal way of reducing your tax bill |
| A legal way of reducing your tax bill |
| For example AB does not declare his income from his night security job |
| For example AB invests surplus income into tax-free securities to avoid paying tax on the interest |

	Tax avoidance	Tax evasion
Characteristic		
Characteristic		

79 An underlying tax is:

   A   the tax deducted at source from the foreign income before it is distributed

   B   the tax on the profits out of which a dividend is paid

   C   the amount of tax relief that can be claimed for double tax relief purposes

   D   the tax paid in the country of residency on foreign income

80 Which TWO of the following are statutory powers that a tax authority may be granted to ensure compliance with tax regulations?

   (i)   Power to arrest individuals

   (ii) Power of entry and search of premises

   (iii) Power to exchange information with other tax authorities

   (iv) Power to confiscate assets of the entity

81 Which of the following is the correct meaning of rollover relief?

   A   A trading loss can be carried forward and used to reduce tax in a future profitable year

   B   A capital loss incurred on the disposal of an asset can be carried forward to a future tax year

   C   An entity ceasing to trade, carrying back a trading loss to set off against previous years' profits

   D   A gain arising from the sale of an asset is deferred provided the entity reinvests the proceeds of the sale in a replacement asset

82 SB operates in Country X and is considering starting business activities in a foreign country.

An entity may conduct a foreign operation through a branch or a subsidiary.

Which of the following is an advantage of SB operating its foreign operation as a subsidiary?

A   A loss made by the foreign operation will be available to the SB group

B   SB will only pay tax on dividends received from its foreign operation

C   All profits/losses overseas will be subject to tax in Country X

D   SB can claim tax depreciation on its foreign operation's assets

83 The government of Country X has estimated the following for the year ended 31 December 20X4:

- Total income tax due $166 billion
- Total income tax expected to be collected $135 billion
- Income tax that will not be collected due to tax evasion $10 billion
- Income tax that will not be collected due to tax avoidance $15 billion

The tax gap for the year to 31 December 20X4 is expected to be:

A $6 billion

B $16 billion

C $21 billion

D $31 billion

84 AB, incorporated in Country X, purchased a non-depreciable asset for $55,000 on 1 January 20X2. AB incurred additional purchase costs of $5,000.

The asset was eventually sold for $210,000 on 31 December 20X5.

The indexation factor from 1 January 20X2 to 31 December 20X5 was 15%.

Tax is charged at 25% on gains.

Calculate the capital tax payable by AB on the disposal of the asset.

$ _____. (Your answer should be rounded down to the nearest $.)

85 **Which TWO of the following is regarded as a direct tax?**

A   Value added tax

B   Capital gains tax

C   Excise duties

D   Property tax

OBJECTIVE TEST QUESTIONS : SECTION 1

86 UI has the following details:

(i) Incorporated in Country A.

(ii) Senior management hold regular board meetings in Country B and exercise control from there, but there are no sales or purchases made in Country B.

(iii) Carries out its main business activities in Country C.

Assume all three countries have double taxation treaties with each other, based on the OECD model tax convention.

In which country/countries will UI be deemed to be resident for tax purposes?

A Country A

B Country B

C Country C

D Countries B and C

87 UV purchased an asset for $50,000 on 1 October 20X6, incurring import duties of $8,000. UV depreciated the asset at 10% per year on a straight line basis.

UV sold the asset for $80,000 on 30 September 20X9, incurring costs of $2,000. The asset was subject to capital gains tax of 25% and the indexation factor from 1 October 20X6 to 30 September 20X9 was 14%.

Calculate the capital tax payable by UV on the disposal of the asset.

$ _____ . (Your answer should be rounded down to the nearest $.)

88 YZ, incorporated in Country X, purchased a non-depreciable asset for $45,000 on 1 January 20X1. YZ incurred additional purchase costs of $5,000.

The asset was eventually sold for $110,000 on 31 December 20X3.

The indexation factor from 1 January 20X1 to 31 December 20X3 was 35%.

Tax is charged on gains at 25%.

Calculate the capital tax payable by YZ on the disposal of the asset.

A $10,625

B $16,250

C $42,500

D $60,000

89 **Complete the sentence below by placing one of the following options in the space.**

An indexation allowance _____ .

| increases a chargeable gain |
| reduces a chargeable gain |
| increases a taxable profit |
| reduces a taxable profit |

SUBJECT F1: FINANCIAL REPORTING

90 In Country Y, A earns $75,000 profit for the year and receives a tax bill for $15,000.

B earns $40,000 profit for the year and receives a tax bill for $8,000.

Country Y's income tax could be said to be a:

A   Regressive tax

B   Proportionate tax

C   Progressive tax

D   Fixed rate tax

91 Place TWO of the following options into the highlighted boxes in the table below to correctly explain the characteristics of transfer pricing.

This results in transactions not taking place at 'arm's length' and profits being effected by the group members
This does not have an effect on individual entity profits for tax purposes
This arises in group situations when either goods are sold inter-company or loans take place at a favourable price
This effect the calculation of the group profit for tax purposes

	Transfer pricing
Characteristic	
Characteristic	

THE REGULATORY ENVIRONMENT OF FINANCIAL REPORTING

92 The IASB's *The Conceptual Framework for Financial Reporting* defines elements of financial statements.

Complete the sentence below by placing one of the following options in the space.

An asset is a _____.

resource controlled by the entity as a result of past events and from which future economic benefits are expected to flow to the entity
present economic resource controlled by the entity as a result of past events

93 According to the IASB's *The Conceptual Framework for Financial Reporting*, what is the objective of financial statements?

Complete the sentence below by placing one of the following options in the space.

The objective of financial reporting is _____.

to prepare ledger accounts for every transaction to enable financial statements to be prepared
to provide information about the reporting entity that is useful to users in making decisions relating to providing resources to the entity
to record transactions in order to produce a trial balance and financial statements
to present the results so that management can make economic decisions and decide how to allocate resources

94 Which of the following is an enhancing qualitative characteristic according to the IASB's *Framework*?

- A Relevance
- B Verifiability
- C Prudence
- D Accruals

95 What is the main function of the IFRS Interpretations Committee?

- A Issuing International Financial Reporting Standards
- B Withdrawing International Financial Reporting Standards
- C Overseeing the development of International Financial Reporting Standards
- D Interpreting the application of International Financial Reporting Standards

96 In the organisation structure for the regulation and supervision of International Accounting Standards, which of the bodies listed below acts as the overall supervisory body?

- A IFRS Foundation
- B International Accounting Standards Board
- C IFRS Advisory Council
- D IFRS Interpretations Committee

97 Which TWO of the following is NOT a topic included in the International Accounting Standards Board's (IASB) *The Conceptual Framework for Financial Reporting*?

- A The objective of financial statements
- B Concepts of capital maintenance
- C Regulatory bodies governing financial statements
- D Measurement of the elements of financial statements
- E The standard setting process

98 The IASB's *The Conceptual Framework for Financial Reporting* defines five elements of financial statements.

Complete the sentence below by placing one of the following options into each of the two spaces.

The elements are assets, liabilities, income, _____ and _____.

expenses	equity
capital	expenditure
losses	profit

99 Which THREE of the following are functions of the IFRS Committee Foundation?

   A   Issuing International Accounting Standards

   B   Approving the annual budget of the IASB and its committees

   C   Enforcing International Accounting Standards

   D   Reviewing the strategy of the IASB

   E   Publishing an annual report on the activities of the IASB

   F   Interpreting International Accounting Standards

100 Complete the sentence below by placing one of the following options into each of the two spaces.

The IASB's *Framework* identifies two methods of capital maintenance which are the _____ concept and the _____ concept.

physical	accruals
going concern	financial
prudence	consistency

101 Complete the sentence below by placing one of the following options into the space.

The IASB's *Framework* identifies the underlying assumption as the_____ concept.

matching	accruals
going concern	faithful representation
prudence	consistency

102 Which of the following gives the best description of the objectives of financial statements as set out by the IASB's *The Conceptual Framework for Financial Reporting*?

   A   To explain to providers of financial capital how an entity creates value over time

   B   To enable an entity to be scrutinised by shareholders and regulators through auditing

   C   To present the assets, liabilities, income, expenses and equity of an entity for utilisation by the users of the financial statements

   D   To provide information about the reporting entity that is useful to users in making decisions relating to providing resources to the entity

103 The IASB's *Conceptual Framework for Financial Reporting* defines a liability as:

   A   an amount owed to another entity

   B   a present obligation arising as a result of past events, the settlement of which is expected to result in an outflow of economic benefits

   C   expenditure that has been incurred but not yet charged to the statement of profit or loss

   D   a present obligation of the entity to transfer an economic resource as a result of past events

OBJECTIVE TEST QUESTIONS : SECTION 1

104 Under the IASB's *The Conceptual Framework for Financial Reporting* the threshold quality of useful financial information is:

A relevance

B reliability

C materiality

D understandability

105 The IASB's *The Conceptual Framework for Financial Reporting* provides definitions of the elements of financial statements. One of the elements defined by the Framework is expenses.

Complete the sentence below by placing one of the following options in the space.

Expenses are decreases in assets or increases in liabilities that result in _____ in equity, other than those relating to distributions to equity participants.

| increases |
| decreases |

106 Which of the following is NOT a function of the IASB?

A Enforcing international financial reporting standards

B Issuing international financial reporting standards

C Approving International Financial Reporting Interpretations Committee's interpretations of international financial reporting standards

D Issuing exposure drafts for public comment

107 Which TWO of the following does the IASB's *Conceptual Framework* NOT cover?

A The format of financial statements

B The objective of financial statements

C Concepts of capital maintenance

D The elements of financial statements

E The users of the financial statements

108 According to the IASB's *The Conceptual Framework for Financial Reporting*, equity is described as:

A the amount paid into the enterprise by the owner

B accumulated profits less amounts withdrawn

C the residual interest in the assets of the entity after deducting all its liabilities

D owner's capital investment in the enterprise

SUBJECT F1: FINANCIAL REPORTING

109 The IASB's *The Conceptual Framework for Financial Reporting* lists two fundamental qualitative characteristics of financial statements, one of which is faithful representation.

Which of the following is NOT a characteristic of faithful representation?

- A Completeness
- B Neutrality
- C Free from error
- D Accruals

110 E, a trainee management accountant, prepares an annual analysis of the performance of all staff, including her own. The analysis is used by the financial director to calculate staff bonuses each year.

According to the CIMA code of ethics for professional accountants which of the threats listed below would apply to E?

- A Advocacy threat
- B Intimidation threat
- C Familiarity threat
- D Self-interest threat

111 Accounting and information disclosure practices are influenced by a variety of factors around the world.

Place THREE of the following options into the highlighted boxes in the table below to correctly identify these factors.

| Social |
| Environmental |
| Economic |
| Political |
| Auditors |

Factors influencing accounting and disclosure

112 Which of the following is a function of the IFRS Foundation?

- A Complete responsibility for the preparation and publication of International Financial Reporting Standards (IFRSs)
- B Approving annually the budget and determining the funding of the International Accounting Standards Board (IASB)
- C To inform the IASB of the views of organisations and individuals on major standard setting projects
- D To review new financial reporting issues not yet covered by an IFRS

113 R, a trainee management accountant is employed by JH. R has prepared the draft annual financial statements for JH and presented them to JH's Chief Executive prior to the executive board meeting. The Chief Executive has told R that the profit reported in the financial statements is too low and must be increased by $500,000 before the financial statements can be approved by the executive board.

Which of the threats listed below would apply to R in this situation, according to the CIMA code of ethics for professional accountants?

A Advocacy threat

B Self-review threat

C Intimidation threat

D Self-interest threat

114 Place THREE of the following options into the highlighted boxes in the table below to correctly explain the functions of the IFRS Advisory Council.

Approving annually the budget and determining the funding of the IASB
To give advice to the IASB on agenda decisions
Review, on a timely basis, new financial reporting issues not specifically addressed in IFRSs
To give advice to the IASB on the priorities in its work
To give any other advice to the IASB or the Trustees
Reviewing annually the strategy of the IASB and its effectiveness

Functions of the IFRS Advisory Council

115 Complete the sentence below by placing one of the following options into each of the two spaces.

The IASB's The Conceptual Framework for Financial Reporting splits qualitative characteristics of useful information into two categories, fundamental and enhancing.

The TWO fundamental qualitative characteristics are _____ and _____.

comparability	faithful representation
relevance	neutral
materiality	understandability

116 The IASB's *Conceptual Framework* sets out measurement bases to use to quantify the value of assets and liabilities. Which of the following is not an acceptable measurement basis outlined by the framework?

A Historical cost

B Value-in-use

C Fair value

D indexed unit value

117 Which of the following bodies is responsible for the approval of interpretations of international financial reporting standards before they are issued?

    A   IASB

    B   IFRS Advisory Council

    C   IFRS Foundation

    D   IFRS Interpretations Committee

118 The IASB's *The Conceptual Framework for Financial Reporting* identifies qualitative characteristics of financial statements.

Which TWO of the following characteristics are NOT fundamental qualitative characteristics according to the IASB's *Framework*?

(i)   Relevance

(ii)   Reliability

(iii)   Faithful representation

(iv)   Comparability

119 C is a small developing country which passed legislation to create a recognised professional accounting body two years ago. At the same time as the accounting body was created, new regulations governing financial reporting requirements of entities were passed. However, there are currently no accounting standards in C.

C's government has asked the new professional accounting body to prepare a report setting out the country's options for developing and implementing a set of high quality local accounting standards. The government request also referred to the work of the IASB and its International Financial Reporting Standards.

Place the following options into the highlighted boxes in the table below to correctly explain ONE advantage and ONE disadvantage of each of the following options. The options cannot be used more than once.

Any standards developed will be specific to C's requirements
Quick to implement
It will not be quick to implement
Standards may not take into account any specific local traditions or variations
Standards should be more relevant to local needs and compliant with International Standards
It will take longer to implement and requires an adequate level of expertise to exist within the country

	Adopting International Financial Reporting Standards (IFRS) as its local standards	Modelling local accounting standards on the IASB's IFRSs, but amending them to reflect local needs and conditions	Develop its own accounting standards with little or no reference to IFRSs
Advantage			
Disadvantage			

120 Place TWO of the following options into the highlighted boxes in the table below to correctly explain the purpose of The Conceptual Framework for Financial Reporting.

Assist the IASB on agenda decisions and priorities in its work
Assist all parties to understand and interpret the Standards
Assist the IASB in the development of future IFRSs and in its review of existing IFRSs
Assist directors when preparing budgets and allocating resources

The purpose of the Framework

121 Generally accepted accounting practice (GAAP) in a country can be based on legislation and accounting standards that are either:

- Very prescriptive in nature; or
- Principle-based.

Place the following options into the highlighted boxes in the table below to correctly explain principle-based accounting standards and prescriptive standards.

The standard would require a certain treatment to be used, regardless of the situation
The standard would be applied using professional judgement
Flexible
Less flexible
Standards should ensure the spirit of the regulations are adhered to
Standards more likely to lead to the letter of the law being followed rather than the spirit

Principle-based accounting standards	Prescriptive accounting standards

122 The IASB's *The Conceptual Framework for Financial Reporting* provides definitions of the elements of financial statements. One of the elements defined by the Framework is income.

Complete the sentence below by placing one of the following options into the spaces provided. Options can be used more than once.

Income is _____ in assets or _____ in liabilities that result in increases in equity, other than those relating to contributions from equity participants.

increases
decreases

SUBJECT F1: FINANCIAL REPORTING

123 Criteria must be met for assets and liabilities to be recognised in an entity's financial statements.

Complete the sentence below by placing one of the following options into each of the spaces.

element	qualitative characteristic
relevant	reasonable
fair value	faithful representation

In order to recognise items in the statement of financial position or statement of profit or loss, The Framework states the following criteria should be satisfied:

- it meets the definition of an _____ of the financial statements
- provides _____ information regarding the particular element
- provides a _____ of the particular element

124 CX, a professional accountant is facing a dilemma. She is working on the preparation of a long term profit forecast required by the local stock market listing regulations prior to a new share issue of equity shares.

At a previous management board meeting, her projections had been criticised by board members as being too pessimistic. She was asked to review her assumptions and increase the profit projections.

She revised her assumptions, but this had only marginally increased the forecast profits.

At yesterday's board meeting the board members had discussed her assumptions and specified new values to be used to prepare a revised forecast. In her view the new values grossly overestimate the forecast profits.

The management board intends to publish the revised forecasts.

Which TWO of following ethical threats does CX face?

A   Self interest

B   Advocacy

C   Familiarity

D   Intimidation

E   Self review

OBJECTIVE TEST QUESTIONS : SECTION 1

125 Place the following options into the highlighted boxes in the table below to correctly show the order a professional accountant should deal with an ethical dilemma.

Report internally to immediate management
Report externally
Remove herself from the situation
Gather evidence and document the problem
Report internally to higher management

	Dealing with an ethical dilemma
1	
2	
3	
4	
5	

126 RS, an employee, prepares monthly management accounting information for XYZ which includes detailed performance data that is used to calculate staff bonuses. Based on information prepared by RS this year's bonuses will be lower than expected.

RS has had approaches from another staff member, who RS has never met before, offering various incentives to make accruals for additional revenue and other reversible adjustments, to enable all staff (including RS) to receive increased or higher bonuses.

Which of the following ethical threats best describes the threat to RS?

- A Advocacy threat
- B Self-review threat
- C Familiarity threat
- D Self-interest threat

127 There are the four main entities that are involved in developing and implementing International Accounting Standards.

Place the following options into the highlighted boxes in the table below to correctly show one role of each of the four entities.

Provides timely guidance on the application and interpretation of IFRSs
Provides strategic advice to the IASB and informs the IASB of public views on major standard setting projects
Governance and fund raising
Responsibility for all technical matters including the preparation and publication of international financial reporting standards

IFRS Foundation	International Accounting Standards Board (IASB)	IFRS Advisory Council	IFRS Interpretations Committee

128 XQ, an employee of ABC, prepares monthly management accounting information for ABC. This information includes detailed performance data that is used to evaluate managers' performance. The directors are considering the closure of some facilities and XQ's management information will be included in the review.

XQ has had approaches from a number of concerned managers offering various incentives to make adjustments to the management accounting information to improve their performance statistics.

Which THREE of following ethical principles does XQ face?

A   Integrity

B   Confidentiality

C   Professional care and due competence

D   Objectivity

E   Neutrality

129 Ace is a management accountant working as part of a small team that has been set up by ZY, his employer, to evaluate tenders submitted for contracts being awarded by ZY.

He has just discovered that one of the other team members accepted large payments in exchange for information, from an entity at the time it was considering tendering. Ace suspects that this may have influenced the winning tender submitted by the entity.

Ace should document the situation and then report it internally to his line manager. If this is unsuccessful what should he do next?

A   Report it to CIMA

B   Report it externally to shareholders

C   Report it internally to higher management

D   Report it externally to a legal advisor

130 Under the current structure of regulatory bodies, which organisation is responsible for reviewing international reporting standards and issuing revised international reporting standards?

A   IFRS Advisory Council

B   IFRS Interpretations Committee

C   International Accounting Standards Board

D   IFRS Foundation

131 Which ONE of the following is NOT a fundamental principle of the CIMA Code of Ethics?

A   Objectivity

B   Integrity

C   Confidentiality

D   Responsibility

132 Which TWO of the following are responsibilities of the IFRS Advisory Council?

(i) Give advice to the IASB on agenda decisions and priorities in its work

(ii) Annually review the strategy of the IASB

(iii) Inform the IASB of the views of the members of the Council on proposed new standards

(iv) Appoint the members of the IASB

133 The IASB's *Conceptual Framework for Financial Reporting* identifies the fundamental and enhancing qualitative characteristics of financial statements.

Place the following options into the highlighted boxes in the table below to correctly show which are the fundamental and enhancing characteristics.

Relevance	Understandability
Comparability	Verifiability
Timeliness	Faithful representation

Fundamental	Enhancing

134 Which of the following is NOT listed as an element of financial statements by the IASB *Conceptual Framework for Financial Reporting*?

A Asset

B Equity

C Profit

D Expenses

135 The IASB's *Conceptual Framework for Financial Reporting* identifies faithful representation as a fundamental qualitative characteristic of financial information.

Which of the following is NOT a characteristic of faithful representation?

A Free from error

B Verifiable

C Neutral

D Complete

SUBJECT F1: FINANCIAL REPORTING

136 Complete the sentence below by placing one of the following options into the space.

The purpose of corporate governance is to protect the _____.

| directors |
| employees |
| shareholders |

137 Complete the sentence below by placing one of the following options into each of the spaces.

Corporate governance is the means by which a company is _____ and _____.

organised	taxed
directed	accounted for
created	controlled

138 The aim of corporate governance initiatives is to ensure that entities are run well in the interests of their shareholders and the wider community.

Which of the following does it NOT include?

A   The necessity for good internal control

B   The necessity for an audit committee

C   Relationships with the external auditors

D   Relationships with the internal auditors

139 There are different approaches to corporate governance, rules-based and principle-approach.

Place the following options into the highlighted boxes in the table below to correctly show the characteristics of each approach.

Comply with the code or explain why	Applied in the UK
Applied in the US	Penalties for transgression
Instils the code into law	Adhere to the spirit rather than the letter of the code

Rules-based	Principle-based

36

OBJECTIVE TEST QUESTIONS : SECTION 1

FINANCIAL STATEMENTS

140 In the statement of cash flow of BKS for the year to 31 December 20X5 the net cash flow from operating activities is to be arrived at by the indirect method.

The following information is relevant:

	$000
Profit before tax	12,044
Depreciation	1,796
Loss on sale of tangible non-current assets	12
Increase in inventories	398
Increase in receivables	144
Increase in payables	468

Calculate the cash generated from operations for the year ended 31 December 20X5.

$ _____. (Your answer should be rounded down to the nearest $000.)

141 At 30 September 20X5, BY had the following balances, with comparatives:

Statement of financial position extracts

As at 30 September	20X5	20X4
	$000	$000
Non-current tangible assets		
Property, plant and equipment	260	180
Equity and reserves		
Property, plant and equipment revaluation reserve	30	10

The statement of profit or loss for the year ended 30 September 20X5 included:

Gain on disposal of an item of equipment	$10,000
Depreciation charge for the year	$40,000

Notes to the accounts:

Equipment disposed of had cost $90,000. The proceeds received on disposal were $15,000.

Calculate the property, plant and equipment purchases that BY would show in its statement of cash flow for the year ended 30 September 20X5, as required by IAS 7 *Statement of Cash Flows*.

$ _____. (Your answer should be rounded down to the nearest $.)

SUBJECT F1: FINANCIAL REPORTING

142 At 1 October 20X4, BK had the following balance:

Accrued interest payable $12,000 credit

During the year ended 30 September 20X5, BK charged interest payable of $41,000 to its statement of profit or loss. The closing balance on accrued interest payable account at 30 September 20X5 was $15,000 credit.

How much interest paid should BK show on its cash flow statement for the year ended 30 September 20X5?

A $38,000

B $41,000

C $44,000

D $53,000

143 There follows extracts from the financial statements of BET for the year to 31 March 20X5 (all figures are in $000).

Extract from the statement of profit or loss

	$000	$000
Profit from operations		1,600
Finance cost		
Interest expense	460	
Interest income	(10)	
		(450)
		1,150

Extracts from the statement of financial position as at 31 March

	20X5	20X4
Current liabilities – interest accrual	560	460

The amount of interest paid that should be included in BET's statement of cash flows for the year ended 31 December 20X5 is:

A $350,000

B $360,000

C $370,000

D $560,000

144 The following balances were extracted from N's financial statements:

Extracts from the statement of financial position as at 31 December

	20X9	20X8
	$000	$000
Current liabilities		
Interest payable	157	133

Extract from statement of profit or loss and other comprehensive income for the year ended 31 December 20X9

	$000
Finance costs	122

The amount of interest paid that should be included in N's statement of cash flows for the year ended 31 December 20X9 is:

A $98,000

B $109,000

C $122,000

D $241,000

145 Which TWO of the following would be shown in a statement of cash flow using the direct method but not in a statement of cash flow using the indirect method of calculating cash generated from operations?

A Cash payments to employees

B Increase/(decrease) in receivables

C Depreciation

D Finance costs

E Cash receipts from customers

146 IAS 7 *Statement of Cash Flows* sets out the three main headings to be used in a statement of cash flows.

Which THREE of the following items would be included under the heading Cash flows from operating activities according to IAS 7?

A Tax paid

B Purchase of investments

C Loss on disposal of machinery

D Purchase of equipment

E Impairment of an asset

F Proceeds from the sale of intangibles

SUBJECT F1: FINANCIAL REPORTING

147 CI purchased equipment on 1 April 20X2 for $100,000. The equipment was depreciated using the reducing balance method at 25% per year. CI's reporting date is 31 March.

Depreciation was charged up to and including 31 March 20X6. At that date, the recoverable amount was $28,000.

Calculate the impairment loss on the equipment according to IAS 36 *Impairment of Assets* for the year to 31 March 20X6.

$ _____ . (Your answer should be rounded to the nearest $.)

148 DOC purchased property for $320,000 exactly 10 years ago. The land included in the price was valued at $120,000. The property was estimated to have a useful economic life of 20 years.

DOC has now had the property revalued (for the first time) by a professional valuer. The total value had increased to $800,000, the land now being valued at $200,000. The useful economic life remained unchanged.

Calculate the amount that should be credited to DOC's revaluation reserve.

$ _____ . (Your answer should be rounded down to the nearest $.)

149 Which of the following gives the best definition of Property, Plant and Equipment, based on the provisions of IAS 16?

    A   Any assets held by an enterprise for more than one accounting period for use in the production or supply of goods or services, for rental to others, or for administrative purposes

    B   Tangible assets held by an enterprise for more than 12 months for use in the production or supply of goods or services, for rental to others, or for administrative purposes

    C   Tangible assets held by an enterprise for more than one accounting period for use in the production or supply of goods or services, for rental to others, or for administrative purposes

    D   Any assets held by an enterprise for more than 12 months for use in the production or supply of goods or services, for rental to others, or for administrative purposes

OBJECTIVE TEST QUESTIONS : SECTION 1

150 JT is registered with its local tax authority and can reclaim value added tax paid on items purchased.

During the year JT purchased a large machine from another country. The supplier invoiced JT as follows:

	$
Cost of basic machine	100,000
Special modifications made to basic design	15,000
Supplier's engineer's time installing and initial testing of machine	2,000
Three years' maintenance and servicing	21,000
	138,000
Value added tax @ 20%	27,600
Total	165,600

Prior to delivery, JT spent $12,000 preparing a heavy duty concrete base for the machine.

Calculate the amount that JT should debit to non-current assets for the cost of the machine.

$ _____. (Your answer should be rounded down to the nearest $.)

151 Which of the following statements is correct?

Statement 1: If the revaluation model is used for property, plant and equipment, revaluations must subsequently be made with sufficient regularity to ensure that the carrying amount does not differ materially from the fair value at each reporting date.

Statement 2: When an item of property, plant and equipment is revalued, there is no requirement that the entire class of assets to which the item belongs must be revalued.

- A   Statement 1 only is correct
- B   Statement 2 only is correct
- C   Both statements are correct
- D   Neither statement is correct

SUBJECT F1: FINANCIAL REPORTING

152 F's year-end is 30 June. F purchased a non-current asset for $50,000 on 1 July 20X2.

Depreciation was provided at the rate of 20% per annum on the straight-line basis. There was no forecast residual value.

On 1 July 20X4, the asset was revalued to $60,000 and then depreciated on a straight-line basis over its remaining useful economic life which was unchanged. On 1 July 20X5, the asset was sold for $35,000.

In addition to the entries in the non-current asset account and provision for depreciation account, which TWO of the following statements correctly record the entries required on disposal of the non-current asset?

A   Debit statement of profit or loss with a loss on disposal of $5,000

B   Credit statement of profit or loss with a gain on disposal of $25,000

C   Transfer $60,000 from revaluation reserve to retained earnings as a movement on reserves

D   Transfer $30,000 from revaluation reserve to retained earnings as a movement on reserves

E   Transfer $30,000 from revaluation reserve to statement of profit or loss

153 Which of the following items would CM recognise as subsequent expenditure on a non-current asset and capitalise it as required by IAS 16 *Property, Plant and Equipment*?

A   CM purchased a furnace five years ago, when the furnace lining was separately identified in the accounting records. The furnace now requires relining at a cost of $200,000. When the furnace is relined it will be able to be used in CM's business for a further five years

B   CM's office building has been badly damaged by a fire. CM intends to restore the building to its original condition at a cost of $250,000

C   CM's delivery vehicle broke down. When it was inspected by the repairers it was discovered that it needed a new engine. The engine and associated labour costs are estimated to be $5,000

D   CM closes its factory for two weeks every year. During this time, all plant and equipment has its routine annual maintenance check and any necessary repairs are carried out. The cost of the current year's maintenance check and repairs was $75,000

154 DS purchased a machine on 1 October 20X2 at a cost of $21,000 with an expected useful economic life of six years, with no expected residual value. DS depreciates its machines using the straight line basis.

The machine has been used and depreciated for three years to 30 September 20X5. New technology was invented in December 20X5, which enabled a cheaper, more efficient machine to be produced; this technology makes DS's type of machine obsolete. The obsolete machine will generate no further economic benefit or have any residual value once the new machines become available. However, because of production delays, the new machines will not be available on the market until 1 October 20X7.

Calculate how much depreciation DS should charge to its statement of profit or loss for the year ended 30 September 20X6, as required by IAS 16 *Property, Plant and Equipment*.

$ _____ . (Your answer should be rounded down to the nearest $.)

OBJECTIVE TEST QUESTIONS : SECTION 1

155 An item of plant and equipment was purchased on 1 April 20X1 for $100,000. At the date of acquisition its expected useful economic life was ten years. Depreciation was provided on a straight line basis, with no residual value.

On 1 April 20X3, the asset was revalued to $95,000. On 1 April 20X4, the useful life of the asset was reviewed and the remaining useful economic life was reduced to five years, a total useful life of eight years.

Calculate the carrying amount at 31 March 20X5, as required by IAS 16 *Property, Plant and Equipment*.

$ _____. (Your answer should be rounded down to the nearest $.)

156 IAS 16 *Property, Plant and Equipment* requires an asset to be measured at cost on its original recognition in the financial statements.

EW used its own staff, assisted by contractors when required, to construct a new warehouse for its own use.

Which of the following costs would NOT be included in attributable costs of the non-current asset?

- A   Clearance of the site prior to work commencing
- B   Professional surveyors' fees for managing the construction work
- C   EW's own staff wages for time spent working on the construction
- D   An allocation of EW's administration costs, based on EW staff time spent on the construction as a percentage of the total staff time

157 GK purchased a piece of development land on 31 October 20X0 for $500,000. GK revalued the land on 31 October 20X4 to $700,000. The latest valuation report, dated 31 October 20X8, values the land at $450,000.

GK has adjusted the land balance shown in non-current assets at 31 October 20X8.

Which of the following shows the correct debit entry in GK's financial statements for the year ended 31 October 20X8?

A	Dr Revaluation reserve	50,000
	Dr Statement of profit or loss	$200,000
B	Dr Revaluation reserve	$250,000
C	Dr Revaluation reserve	$200,000
	Dr Statement of profit or loss	$50,000
D	Dr Statement of profit or loss	$250,000

SUBJECT F1: FINANCIAL REPORTING

158 On 1 July 20X4, Experimenter opened a chemical reprocessing plant at a cost of $10 million. The plant was due to be active for five years until 30 June 20X9, when it would be decommissioned. At 1 July 20X4, the costs of decommissioning the plant were estimated to be $4 million. The company considers that a discount rate of 12% is appropriate for the calculation of a present value, and the discount factor at 12% for Year 5 is 0.567.

What is the carrying amount of the plant as at the year ended 30 June 20X5? Answers are quoted in $000s

- A $8,000
- B $9,814
- C $12,268
- D $14,000

159 An entity purchased an item of property for $6 million on 1 July 20X3. The value of the land was $1 million and the buildings $5 million. The expected life of the building was 50 years and its residual value nil. On 30 June 20X5 the property was revalued to $7 million (land $1.24 million, buildings $5.76 million). On 30 June 20X7, the property was sold for $6.8 million.

Which TWO of the following are true regarding the treatment of the disposal of the property for the year to 30 June 20X7?

- A Gain on disposal of $40,000
- B Gain on disposal of $200,000
- C Gain on disposal of $84,800
- D Release the revaluation reserve of $1,240,000
- E Release the revaluation reserve of $1,200,000

160 On 1 January Year 1, an entity purchased an item of equipment costing $76,000. The asset is depreciated using the reducing balance method, at a rate of 20% each year. After three years, an impairment review establishes that the asset has a value in use of $30,000 and a disposal value (less selling costs) of $27,000.

Calculate the amount of the impairment loss that should be written off in the statement of profit or loss for the year to 31 December Year 3.

$ _____ .(Your answer should be rounded down to the nearest $.)

161 The information below refers to three non-current assets of IDLE as at 31 March 20X5:

| | A | B | C |
	$000	$000	$000
Carrying amount	200	300	240
Net selling price	220	250	200
Value in use	240	260	180

What is the total impairment loss?

- A $40,000
- B $80,000
- C $90,000
- D $110,000

OBJECTIVE TEST QUESTIONS : SECTION 1

162 The following measures relate to a non-current asset:

(i) carrying amount $20,000

(ii) net realisable value $18,000

(iii) value in use $22,000

(iv) replacement cost $50,000.

The recoverable amount of the asset is:

A $18,000

B $20,000

C $22,000

D $50,000

163 Diva has tangible non-current assets in its statement of financial position at 31 December 20X4 and 31 December 20X5 as follows:

The following information is also available:

1 During the year, machines were sold for net sales proceeds of $20,000. The machines originally cost $125,000 and accumulated depreciation on the assets at the date of disposal was $111,000.

2 Assets under construction refer to a contract, started in November 20X4, to build and supply C with new machinery. The machinery was installed and testing was completed by 31 September 20X5. Production began early October 20X5. The balance on the assets under construction account was transferred to the plant and machinery account on 31 December 20X5. The amount transferred was $350,000.

Place the following options into the highlighted boxes in the table on the next page to complete the disclosure note for property, plant and equipment for the year ended 31 December 20X5. The options can be used more than once and not all options have to be used.

(20)	0	772	(350)
(125)	(111)	1,459	125
145	403	1,550	111
350	9,876	863	20
1,240	890	297	2,115

SUBJECT F1: FINANCIAL REPORTING

Property, plant and equipment note 31 December 20X5

	Land	Buildings	Plant and machinery	Under construction	Total
Cost/valuation	$000	$000	$000	$000	$000
Balance at 1 January 20X5	2,743	3,177	1,538	53	7,511
Revaluation of assets	375	–	–	0	375
Disposal of assets	–	–		–	
Transfers	–	–			0
Additions	402	526			
Balance at 31 December 20X5	3,520	3,703	2,653		
Depreciation					
Balance at 1 January 20X5	–	612	671	–	1,283
Disposal of assets	–	–		–	
Depreciation for the year	–	75	212	–	287
Balance at 31 December 20X5	0	687		0	
Carrying amount 31 December 20X5	3,520	3,016	1,881	0	8,417
Carrying amount 31 December 20X4	2,743	2,565	867	53	6,228

164 Neville has only two items of inventory on hand at its reporting date.

Item 1 – Materials costing $24,000 bought for processing and assembly for a customer under a 'one off' order which is expected to produce a high profit margin. Since buying this material, the cost price has fallen to $20,000.

Item 2 – A machine constructed for another customer for a contracted price of $36,000. This has recently been completed at a cost of $33,600. It has now been discovered that, in order to meet certain health and safety regulations, modifications at an extra cost of $8,400 will be required. The customer has agreed to meet half the extra cost.

Calculate the total value of these two items of inventory in the statement of financial position.

$ _____ .(Your answer should be rounded down to the nearest $)

165 IAS 2 *Inventories* specifies expenses that should be included in year-end inventory values.

Which THREE of the following are allowable by IAS 2 as expenses that should be included in the cost of finished goods inventories?

- A Marketing and selling overhead
- B Variable production overhead
- C General management overhead
- D Accounting and finance overhead allocated to production
- E Cost of delivering raw materials to the factory
- F Abnormal increase in overhead charges caused by unusually low production levels due to the exceptionally hot weather

166 Which of the following would be treated as a non-adjusting event after the reporting date, as required by IAS 10 *Events after the Reporting Period*, in the financial statements of AN for the period ended 31 January 20X5? The financial statements were approved for publication on 15 May 20X5.

  A   Notice was received on 31 March 20X5 that a major customer of AN had ceased trading and was unlikely to make any further payments

  B   Inventory items at 31 January 20X5, original cost $30,000, were sold in April 20X5 for $20,000

  C   During 20X4, a customer commenced legal action against AN. At 31 January 20X5, legal advisers were of the opinion that AN would lose the case, so AN recorded a liability of $200,000 for the damages claimed by the customer. On 27 April 20X5, the court awarded damages of $250,000 to the customer

  D   There was a fire on 2 May 20X5 in AN's main warehouse which destroyed 50% of AN's total inventory

167 Using the requirements set out in IAS 10 *Events after the Reporting Period*, which of the following would be classified as an adjusting event after the reporting period in financial statements ended 31 March 20X4 that were approved by the directors on 31 August 20X4?

  A   A reorganisation of the enterprise, proposed by a director on 31 January 20X4 and agreed by the Board on 10 July 20X4

  B   A strike by the workforce which started on 1 May 20X4 and stopped all production for 10 weeks before being settled

  C   A claim on an insurance policy for damage caused by a fire in a warehouse on 1 January 20X4. No record had been made for the receipt of insurance money at 31 March 20X4 as it was uncertain that any money would be paid. The insurance enterprise settled with a payment of $1.5 million on 1 June 20X4

  D   The enterprise had made large export sales to the USA during the year. The year-end receivables included $2 million for amounts outstanding that were due to be paid in US dollars between 1 April 20X4 and 1 July 20X4. By the time these amounts were received, the exchange rate had moved in favour of the enterprise and the equivalent of $2.5 million was actually received

168 GD's financial reporting period is 1 September 20X7 to 31 August 20X8.

Which TWO of the following would be classified as a non-adjusting event according to IAS 10 *Events after the Reporting Period*?

Assume all amounts are material and that GD's financial statements have not yet been approved for publication.

A   On 30 October 20X8, GD received a communication stating that one of its customers had ceased trading and gone into liquidation. The balance outstanding at 31 August 20X8 was unlikely to be paid

B   At 31 August 20X8, GD had not included any impact for an outstanding legal action against the local government for losses suffered as a result of incorrect enforcement of local business regulations. On 5 November 20X8, the court awarded GD $50,000 damages

C   On 1 October 20X8, GD made a share issue at a price of $1.75

D   At 31 August 20X8, GD had an outstanding insurance claim of $150,000. On 10 October 20X8, the insurance company informed GD that it would pay $140,000 as settlement

E   On 10 October 20X8 GD announced a plan to acquire DE in the next 12 months

169 **Which of the following material items would be classified as a non-adjusting event in HL's financial statements for the year ended 31 December 20X8 according to IAS 10 *Events after the Reporting Period*?**

HL's financial statements were approved for publication on 8 April 20X9.

A   On 1 March 20X9, HL's auditors discovered that, due to an error during the count, the closing inventory had been undervalued by $250,000

B   Lightning struck one of HL's production facilities on 31 January 20X9 and caused a serious fire. The fire destroyed half of the factory and its machinery. Output was severely reduced for six months

C   One of HL's customers commenced court action against HL on 1 December 20X8. At 31 December 20X8, HL did not know whether the case would go against it or not. On 1 March 20X9, the court found against HL and awarded damages of $150,000 to the customer

D   On 15 March 20X9, HL was advised by the liquidator of one of its customers that it was very unlikely to receive any payments for the balance of $300,000 that was outstanding at 31 December 20X8

OBJECTIVE TEST QUESTIONS : SECTION 1

170 DT's final dividend for the year ended 31 October 20X5 of $150,000 was declared on 1 February 20X6 and paid in cash on 1 April 20X6. The financial statements were approved on 31 March 20X6.

Which TWO of the following statements reflect the correct treatment of the dividend?

- A The payment clears an accrued liability set up in the statement of financial position as at 31 October 20X5
- B The dividend is shown as a deduction in the statement of profit or loss for the year ended 31 October 20X6
- C The dividend is shown as an accrued liability in the statement of financial position as at 31 October 20X6
- D The $150,000 dividend was shown in the notes to the financial statements at 31 October 20X5
- E The dividend is shown as a deduction in the statement of changes in equity for the year ended 31 October 20X6

171 IAS 10 *Events after the Reporting Period* distinguishes between adjusting and non-adjusting events.

Place the following options into the highlighted boxes in the table below to correctly show which of the following items are adjusting events and which are non-adjusting events.

A dispute with workers caused all production to cease six weeks after the reporting date
A month after the reporting date XS's directors decided to cease production of one of its three product lines and to close the production facility
One month after the reporting date a court determined a case against XS and awarded damages of $50,000 to one of XS's customers. XS had expected to lose the case and had set up a liability of $30,000 at the reporting date
Three weeks after the reporting date a fire destroyed XS's main warehouse facility and most of its inventory
One month after the year end XS's main customer goes into liquidation owing XS a substantial amount of money
XS discovers a material error in the closing inventory value one month after the reporting date

Adjusting events	Non-adjusting events

SUBJECT F1: FINANCIAL REPORTING

172 BN has an asset that was classified as held for sale at 31 March 20X2. The asset had a carrying amount of $900 and a fair value of $800. The cost of disposal was estimated to be $50.

According to IFRS 5 *Non-current Assets Held for Sale and Discontinued Operations*, which of the following values should be used for the asset in BN's statement of financial position as at 31 March 20X2?

- A $750
- B $800
- C $850
- D $900

173 IAS 1 *Presentation of Financial Statements* encourages an analysis of expenses to be presented on the face of the statement of profit or loss. The analysis of expenses must use a classification based on either the nature of expense, or its function, within the entity.

Which TWO of the following would be disclosed on the face of the statement of profit or loss if a manufacturing entity uses analysis based on function?

- A Raw materials and consumables used
- B Distribution costs
- C Employee benefit costs
- D Cost of sales
- E Depreciation and amortisation expense

174 Which of the following must be presented on the face of the statement of profit or loss?

- (i) Finance charges
- (ii) Profits, gains and losses relating to discontinued operations

- A (i) only
- B (ii) only
- C Both (i) and (ii)
- D Neither

175 Which of the following is NOT required by IAS 1 as an item to include in the notes to the accounts?

- A A statement that the entity is a going concern
- B A statement of compliance with International Financial Reporting Standards
- C The dividends declared or proposed before the publication of the financial statements but not included in the statements as a distribution to shareholders in the period
- D The key sources of estimation uncertainty in the financial statements

176 IAS 1 *Presentation of Financial Statements* requires some of the items to be disclosed on the face of the financial statements and others to be disclosed in the notes.

Which TWO of the following have to be shown on the face of the statement of profit or loss, rather than in the notes?

A   Depreciation

B   Revenue

C   Closing inventory

D   Finance cost

E   Dividends

177 An entity undertakes a revaluation of its freehold property during the current period. The revaluation results in a significant surplus over carrying amount.

In which of the components of the current period financial statements required by IAS 1 would the revaluation surplus appear?

A   Statement of financial position and statement of changes in equity

B   Statement of changes in equity and statement of cash flow

C   Statement of financial position and statement of profit or loss

D   Statement of financial position and statement of cash flow

178 WZ is an assistant accountant with ABC. On 31 March 20X1 ABC decided to sell a property. This property was correctly classified as held for sale in accordance with IFRS 5 *Non-current Assets Held For Sale and Discontinued Operations*.

In its draft financial statements, ABC has written down the property by $3.4 million. The write down was charged to the statement of profit or loss for the year ended 31 August 20X1. The draft financial statements showed a loss of $1.3 million for the year to 31 August 20X1.

Which TWO of the following statements correctly show how WZ should treat the asset?

A   The asset should be shown under PPE until the asset is sold

B   The asset should continue to be depreciated until it is sold

C   The asset should be shown separately under assets held for sale

D   Depreciation should cease at 31 March 20X1

E   Depreciation should cease at 31 August 20X1

179 An entity decided to sell a property. This property was correctly classified as held for sale in accordance with IFRS 5 *Non-current Assets Held For Sale and Discontinued Operations*. When the management board reviewed the draft financial statements, the board members were unhappy that the draft statements showed a loss on the asset and decided that the property should continue to be shown under non-current assets at its previous carrying amount.

Which TWO of the following ethical principles are faced if the entity's finance director follows the management board's advice?

A   Integrity

B   Confidentiality

C   Professional behaviour

D   Objectivity

E   Reliability

180 MN obtained a licence free of charge from the government to dig and operate a gold mine.

On the 31 October 20X9 there was a massive earthquake in the area and MN's mine shaft was badly damaged. It is estimated that the mine will be closed for at least six months and will cost $1 million to repair.

How should MN treat the effects of the earthquake in its financial statements for the year ended 31 August 20X9 in accordance with IAS 10 *Events after the Reporting Period*?

A   Treat as an adjusting event with a disclosure note

B   Treat as a non-adjusting event with a disclosure note

C   Treat as a non-adjusting event without a disclosure note

D   Treat as an adjusting event without a disclosure note

181 On 1 September 20X7, the Directors of EK decided to sell an asset.

The asset was available for immediate sale, but EK had not succeeded in disposing of the asset by 31 October 20X7. EK identified a potential buyer for the asset, but negotiations were at an early stage. The Directors of EK are certain that the sale will be completed by 31 August 20X8.

The asset's carrying value at 31 August 20X7 was $443,000.

The asset has been valued at $423,000, comprising:

EK's directors have estimated that EK will incur consultancy and legal fees for the disposal of $25,000.

Place FOUR of the following options into the highlighted boxes in the table below to correctly show the correct treatment of the discontinued operation according to IFRS 5 *Non-current Assets Held for Sale and Discontinued Operations*, for the year ended 31 October 20X7.

The assets have not met the criteria of an asset held for sale
The assets have met the criteria of an asset held for sale
EK should continue to show the assets in their normal categories in the statement of financial position
The assets should be shown separately as assets held for sale in the statement of financial position
The assets should be valued at $443,000
The assets should be valued at $423,000
The assets should be valued at $398,000
Impairment of $45,000 should be treated as an expense to the statement of profit or loss
Impairment of $20,000 should be treated as an expense to the statement of profit or loss
There is no impairment at the year ended 31 October 20X7

Treatment of the held for sale asset

182 Extracts from CFQ's Statement of financial position at 31 March 20X3, with comparatives appear below:

	31 March 20X3	31 March 20X2
	$ million	$ million
Property, plant and equipment	635	645

During the year to 31 March 20X3, CFQ sold property, plant and equipment for $45m. It had originally cost $322m and had a carrying amount of $60m at the date of disposal.

CFQ's statement of profit or loss for the year ended 31 March 20X3 included:

- depreciation of property, plant and equipment of $120m

Calculate the purchases of property, plant and equipment to be shown in the investing activities section of the statement of cash flow for the year ended 31 March 20X3, in accordance with IAS 7 *Statement of Cash Flows*.

$ _____. (Your answer should be rounded down to the nearest $ million)

183 DV purchased a building on 1 September 20W6. The building cost $200,000 and had an economic life of 20 years. DV's accounting policies are to revalue buildings every five years and depreciate them over their economic lives on the straight line basis. DV does not make an annual transfer from revaluation reserve to retained profits for excess depreciation.

DV received the following external valuations in relation to the building:

31 August 20X1	$180,000
31 August 20X6	$100,000

Complete the sentence below by placing one of the following options into each of the spaces.

DV will _____ for the impact of the revaluation of the building on 31 August 20X6.

- record an expense in the profit or loss
- reduce the revaluation reserve
- increase the revaluation reserve

184 VD purchased a building on 1 September 20W6. The building B cost $120,000 and had a useful economic life of 15 years. VD's accounting policies are to revalue buildings every five years and depreciate them over their useful economic lives on the straight line basis. VD does not make an annual transfer from revaluation reserve to retained profits for excess depreciation.

VD received the following valuations from its professionally qualified external valuer:

31 August 20X1	Building B	$75,000
31 August 20X6	Building B	$30,000

Calculate the gain or impairment arising on the revaluation of Building B for the year ended 31 August 20X6.

$ _____. (Your answer should be rounded down to the nearest $)

185 Extracts from SF's statement of financial position at 31 March 20X3, with comparatives, are shown below:

	20X3	20X2
Equity	$000	$000
Ordinary shares	460	400
Share premium	82	70
Revaluation reserve	44	24
Retained earnings	273	246

Calculate the proceeds from the share issue to be shown in the financing activities section of the statement of cash flow for the year ended 31 March 20X3.

$ _____. (Your answer should be rounded down to the nearest $)

OBJECTIVE TEST QUESTIONS : SECTION 1

186 Extracts from FS's statement of financial position at 31 December 20X3, with comparatives, are shown below:

	20X3	20X2
Non-current liabilities		
Long term borrowings	129	105

During the year ended 31 December 20X3, SF's transactions included the following:

(i) Repaid $25,000 of its long term borrowings during the year.

What would be the impact of the loans within the financing activities section of the statement of cash flow for the year ended 31 December 20X3?

- A Net outflow of $24,000
- B Net inflow of $24,000
- C Outflow of $25,000 and inflow of $49,000
- D Outflow of $49,000 and inflow of $25,000

187 AH owns three hotels. It has employed a firm of surveyors to revalue some of its properties during the past year. The directors have decided that the valuations should be incorporated into the entity's financial statements.

This is the first time that such a revaluation has taken place and the accountant responsible for the preparation of the non-current asset note in the statement of financial position is unsure of the correct treatment of the amounts involved. The entity's year end is 30 September 20X4.

The accountant has extracted the following table from the report prepared by the surveyors:

	Original cost	Depreciation to 30 September 20X3	Market value at 1 January 20X4
	$000	$000	$000
Hotel G	400	96	650
Hotel H	750	56	820
Hotel K	500	70	320

What would be the balance on the revaluation reserve at 30 September 20X4?

- A $362,000
- B $472,000
- C $140,000
- D $320,000

188 Complete the sentence below by placing one of the following options into each of the spaces. The options can be used more than once and not all options have to be used.

An asset held for sale is an asset which is available for _____ sale in its present condition, and the sale is _____. This could be proven by meeting certain conditions, two of which are that there is an _____ to locate a buyer and that the asset is being actively marketed at a _____ price.

active programme	reasonable
immediate	highly probable

SUBJECT F1: FINANCIAL REPORTING

189 Which THREE of the following are the main benefits, to users of the accounts, of including a statement of cash flows in published financial statements?

- A   It can help users assess the liquidity and solvency of an entity
- B   It can help to identify the financial position of the entity
- C   It can help highlight where cash is being generated and where it is being spent
- D   It helps users assess financial adaptability
- E   It can help to identify the financial performance of the entity
- F   It helps to show inflows and outflows in three sections

---

Data for Questions 190 to 194

BI owns a building which it uses as its offices, warehouse and garage. The land is carried as a separate non-current tangible asset at the reporting date.

BI has a policy of regularly revaluing its non-current tangible assets. The original cost of the building in October 20X2 was $1,000,000; it was assumed to have a remaining useful life of 20 years at that date, with no residual value. The building was revalued on 30 September 20X4 by a professional valuer at $1,800,000.

BI also owns a machine, which it acquired on 1 October 20X0 for $500,000. The machine is being depreciated straight line over 10 years.

The economic climate had deteriorated during 20X5, causing BI to carry out an impairment review of its assets at 30 September 20X5. BI's building was valued at a recoverable amount of $1,500,000 on 30 September 20X5 by an independent valuer. A specialist valued BI's machine at a market value of $230,000 on the same date.

BI's management accountant calculated that the machine's value in use at 30 September 20X5 was $150,000.

---

190 How is the machine valued in the statement of financial position for the year ended 30 September 20X5?

- A $250,000
- B $200,000
- C $230,000
- D $150,000

191 What amount should be credited to the revaluation reserve on 30 September 20X4 for the revaluation of the building?

- A $800,000
- B $900,000
- C $950,000
- D $850,000

192 Calculate the depreciation charge for the building for the year ended 30 September 20X5.

$ _____. (Your answer should be rounded down to the nearest $)

OBJECTIVE TEST QUESTIONS : SECTION 1

193 Which of the following statements explains the treatment of the revaluation of the building on 30 September 20X5?

    A   Debit the revaluation reserve with $300,000

    B   Debit the statement of profit or loss with $300,000

    C   Debit the revaluation reserve with $200,000

    D   Debit the statement of profit or loss with $200,000

194 Calculate the depreciation charge for the building for the year ended 30 September 20X6.

$ _____ . (Your answer should be rounded down to the nearest $)

195 CR enters into a lease on 1 January 20X1 for a machine with a fair value of $235,000. CR will make annual payments in arrears of $70,000 over the four year lease term. The rate implicit in the lease is 9%.

Calculate the finance cost that should be recognised in the statement of profit or loss for the year ended 31 December 20X2 (the second year of the lease).

196 DF enters into a 10 year lease arrangement on 30 June 20X1 for portable fitness monitoring devices to grant to its employees as part of its internal wellbeing and corporate responsibility programme. Annual rental payments of $125,000 are to be paid however, as an incentive to the lessee, the first 12 months are rent free. The lease was considered to be for low value items by DF.

Calculate the charge to DF's statement of profit or loss in respect of the lease for the year ended 31 December 20X1.

197 LD enters into a lease on 1 January 20X1. Initial direct costs are $1,000. The lease term is five years and the interest rate implicit in the lease is 7%. The annual lease payments are $110,000 in arrears.

The non-current liability in respect of the above lease at 31 December 20X1 is:

    A $288,650

    B $290,312

    C $372,570

    D $373,890

SUBJECT F1: FINANCIAL REPORTING

198 During the year ended 30 September 20X4 Hyper entered into two lease transactions.

On 1 October 20X3, Hyper made a payment of $90,000 being the first of five equal annual payments under a lease for an item of plant. The lease has an implicit interest rate of 10% and the present value of the total lease payments on 1 October 20X3 was $340,000.

On 1 January 20X4, Hyper made a payment of $18,000 for a one-year lease of an item of equipment.

What amount in total would be charged to Hyper's statement of profit or loss for the year ended 30 September 20X4 in respect of the above transactions?

- A $108,000
- B $111,000
- C $106,500
- D $115,500

199 Z entered into a five year lease agreement on 1 November 20X2, paying $10,975 per annum, commencing on 31 October 20X3. The present value of the lease payments was $45,000 and the interest rate implicit in the lease was 7%.

What is the amount to be shown within non-current liabilities at 31 October 20X3?

- A $26,200
- B $28,802
- C $37,175
- D $36,407

200 IFRS 16 *Leases* permits certain assets to be exempt from the recognition treatment for right-of-use assets.

Which of the following assets leased to an entity would be permitted to be exempt?

- A A used motor vehicle with an original cost of $15,000 and a current fair value of $700, leased for 24 months
- B A new motor vehicle with a cost of $15,000, leased for 24 months
- C A new motor vehicle with a cost of $15,000, leased for 24 months, to be rented to customers on a daily rental basis
- D A new motor vehicle with a cost of $15,000, leased for 12 months

201 On 1 January 20X3 Rabbit acquires a new machine with an estimated useful life of 6 years under the following agreement:

An initial payment of $13,760 will be payable immediately

Five further annual payments of $20,000 will be due, commencing 1 January 20X3

The interest rate implicit in the lease is 8%

The present value of the lease payments, excluding the initial payment, is $86,240

What will be recorded in Rabbit's financial statements at 31 December 20X4 in respect of the lease liability?

	Finance cost	Non-current liability	Current liability
A	4,123	35,662	20,000
B	5,299	51,539	20,000
C	5,312	51,712	20,000
D	5,851	43,709	15,281

202 On 1 April 20X7 Pigeon entered into a five-year lease agreement for a machine with an estimated life of 7 years. Which of the following conditions would require the machine to be depreciated over 7 years?

- A Pigeon has the option to extend the lease for two years at a market-rate rental
- B Pigeon has the option to purchase the asset at market value at the end of the lease
- C Ownership of the asset passes to Pigeon at the end of the lease period
- D Pigeon's policy for purchased assets is to depreciate over 7 years

203 Owl leases an asset with an estimated useful life of 6 years for an initial period of 5 years, and an optional secondary period of 2 years during which a nominal rental will be payable. The present value of the initial period lease payments is $87,000.

What will be the carrying amount of the asset in Owl's statement of financial position at the end of the second year of the lease?

$_____

204 On 1 October 20X3, Fresco acquired an item of plant under a five-year lease agreement. The agreement had an implicit interest rate of 10% and required annual rentals of $6 million to be paid on 30 September each year for five years. The present value of the annual rental payments was $23 million.

What would be the current liability for the leased plant in Fresco's statement of financial position as at 30 September 20X4?

- A $19,300,000
- B $4,070,000
- C $5,000,000
- D $3,850,000

SUBJECT F1: FINANCIAL REPORTING

205 Which of the following would not be included within the initial cost of a right-of-use asset?

- A Installation cost of the asset
- B Estimated cost of dismantling the asset at the end of the lease period
- C Payments made to the lessor before commencement of the lease
- D Total lease rentals payable under the lease agreement

MANAGING CASH AND WORKING CAPITAL

206 If an entity regularly fails to pay its suppliers by the normal due dates, it may lead to a number of problems.

Which TWO of the following could arise as a result of exceeding suppliers' trade credit terms?

- (i) having insufficient cash to settle trade payables
- (ii) difficulty in obtaining credit from new suppliers
- (iii) reduction in credit rating
- (iv) settlement of trade receivables may be delayed.

207 A conservative policy for managing working capital is one where:

- A low levels of working capital are held
- B a high risk of liquidity problems exist but high returns can be achieved
- C a longer working capital cycle would be expected
- D a middle group between risk management and achieving returns is adopted

208 ABC has produced the following sales forecast:

	$000
January	750
February	760
March	770
April	780
May	790
June	800

Currently 20% of customers pay in cash. Of the credit customers (excluding those who become irrecoverable debts), 60% pay in one month, 30% pay in two months and 10% in three months. Irrecoverable debts are 2%. This payment pattern is expected to continue.

Calculate the forecast cash receipts for April.

$ _____. (Your answer should be rounded down to the nearest $.)

OBJECTIVE TEST QUESTIONS : SECTION 1

209 In October, a company made credit purchases of $18,000 and credit sales of $24,000. All sales are made on the basis of cost plus 25%.

Calculate how much the working capital will increase by in October as a result of these transactions.

$ _____. (Your answer should be rounded down to the nearest $)

210 The following items have been extracted from an entity's budget for next month:

	$
Sales on credit	240,000
Expected increase in inventory next month	20,000
Expected decrease in trade receivables next month	12,000

Calculate the budgeted receipt from trade receivables next month.

$ _____. (Your answer should be rounded down to the nearest $.)

211 DY had a balance outstanding on trade receivables at 30 September 20X6 of $68,000. Forecast credit sales for the next six months are $250,000 and customers are expected to return goods with a sales value of $2,500.

Based on past experience, within the next six months DY expects to collect $252,100 cash and to write off as irrecoverable debts 5% of the balance outstanding at 30 September 20X6.

Calculate DY's forecast trade receivables days outstanding at 31 March 20X7.

_____ days. (Your answer should be rounded down to the nearest day.)

212 A company has annual sales of $40 million, annual cost of sales of $30 million and makes annual purchases of $15 million. Its statement of financial position includes among assets and liabilities the following:

Trade receivables	$4 million
Trade payables	$3 million
Inventory	$8 million

What is its working capital cycle?

A 206.5 days

B 60.8 days

C 36.5 days

D 97.3 days

213 XYZ's annual sales are $100m of which 95% are made on credit. Receivables at the beginning of the year were $10 million and at the end of the year total receivables were $12 million. 10% of receivables were non-trade related.

What is XYZ's average collection period?

A 36.5 days

B 40 days

C 38 days

D 46 days

SUBJECT F1: FINANCIAL REPORTING

214 DY's trade receivables balance at 1 April 20X6 was $22,000. DY's statement of profit or loss showed revenue from credit sales of $290,510 during the year ended 31 March 20X7.

DY's trade receivables days at 31 March 20X7 were 49 days.

Assume DY's sales occur evenly throughout the year and that all balances outstanding at 1 April 20X6 have been received.

Also, it should be assumed all sales are on credit, there were no irrecoverable debts and no trade discount was given.

How much cash did DY receive from its customers during the year to 31 March 20X7?

- A $268,510
- B $273,510
- C $312,510
- D $351,510

215 The following items were extracted from an entity's budget for next month:

	$
Purchases on credit	360,000
Expected decrease in inventory during the month	12,000
Expected increase in trade payables during the month	15,000

Calculate the budgeted payment to trade creditors for the month.

$ _____. (Your answer should be rounded down to the nearest $)

216 The trial balance of EH at 31 October 20X7 showed trade receivables of $82,000 before adjustments.

On 1 November 20X7 EH discovered that one of its customers had ceased trading and was very unlikely to pay any of its outstanding balance of $12,250.

On the same date EH carried out an assessment of the collectability of its other trade receivable balances. Using its knowledge of its customers and past experience EH determined that the remaining trade receivables had suffered a 3% impairment at 31 October 20X7.

What is EH's balance of trade receivables, as at 31 October 20X7?

- A $66,202
- B $67,290
- C $67,657
- D $79,540

217 EV had trade payables outstanding of 50 days at 31 October 20X7.

EV's trade payables were $42,000 at 1 November 20X6.

During the year to 31 October 20X7, EV's credit purchases were $351,534.

Assume purchases and sales accrue evenly throughout the year and use a 365-day year. Further assume that there were no goods returned to suppliers and EV claimed no discounts.

Calculate the amount EV paid to its credit suppliers during the year to 31 October 20X7.

$ _____. (Your answer should be rounded down to the nearest $)

OBJECTIVE TEST QUESTIONS : SECTION 1

218 DX had the following balances in its trial balance at 30 September 20X6:

Trial balance extract at 30 September 20X6

	$000	$000
Revenue		2,400
Cost of sales	1,400	
Inventories	360	
Trade receivables	290	
Trade payables		190
Cash and cash equivalents	95	

Calculate the length of DX's working capital cycle at 30 September 20X6.

_____ days. (Your answer should be rounded down to the nearest day.)

219 An entity commenced business on 1 April 20X2. Revenue in April 20X2 was $20,000, but this is expected to increase at 2% a month. Credit sales amount to 60% of total sales. The credit period allowed is one month. Irrecoverable debts are expected to be 3% of credit sales, but other customers are expected to pay on time. Cash sales represent the other 40% of revenue.

Calculate the cash expected to be received in May 20X2.

$ _____ .(Your answer should be rounded down to the nearest $)

220 Which of the following is LEAST likely to characterise overtrading?

    A   Increased borrowing

    B   Increased cash balances

    C   Increased turnover

    D   Reduced working capital

221 Complete the sentence below by placing one of the following options into the space.

An aged trade creditor's analysis (aged trade payables analysis) is _____.

a listing of trade payables by date of invoicing
a listing of trade payables with whom you are in arrears
the proportion of purchases by value which are overdue
a breakdown of trade payables according to length of time elapsing since the purchase was made

SUBJECT F1: FINANCIAL REPORTING

222 FGH requires a rate of return of 12.85% each year.

Two of FGH's suppliers, P and Q, are offering the following terms for immediate cash settlement:

Supplier	Cash settlement discount	Normal settlement period
P	1%	1 month
Q	2%	2 months

Which of the discounts should be accepted to achieve the required rate of return?

A   The discounts offered by both P and Q

B   The discount offered by P only

C   The discount offered by Q only

D   Neither of them

223 WM's major supplier, INT, supplies electrical tools and is one of the largest companies in the industry, with international operations. Deliveries from INT are currently made monthly, and are constant throughout the year. Delivery and invoicing both occur in the last week of each month.

Details of the credit terms offered by INT are as follows:

Normal credit period	Cash discount	Average monthly purchases
40 days	2% for settlement in 10 days	$100,000

WM always takes advantage of the cash discount from INT.

Calculate the annual rate of interest implied in the cash discount offered by INT. Assume a 365-day year.

_____ %. (Your answer should be rounded to two decimal places)

224 What are the THREE main services provided by a without recourse factor?

A   Sales ledger administration

B   Assistance in the creditworthiness of customers

C   Credit insurance

D   Advice on credit control policies

E   Factor finance

F   Training of sales ledger administration staff

225 Complete the sentence below by placing one of the following options into the space.

Invoice discounting normally involves _____.

offering a cash discount for early settlement of invoices
selling an invoice to a discount house at a profit
selling an individual invoice for cash to a factor organisation at a discount
writing off an invoice, partly or in total, as an irrecoverable debt

226 XYZ has $1 million to invest for one year. It can lock it away at a fixed rate of 7% for the full year, or invest at 6.5% for a three-month term, speculating on an increase in interest rates. Assume the rate available increases to 7.5% after three months and XYZ invests at this rate for the rest of the year.

By how much is XYZ better off from its gamble on interest rates?

- A $2,500
- B $12,836
- C $73,414
- D $3,414

227 After a bill of exchange has been accepted, there are a number of possible actions that the drawer could take.

Which of the following is NOT a possible course of action?

- A Ask the customer for immediate payment
- B Discount the bill with a bank
- C Hold the bill until the due date and then present it for payment
- D Use the bill to settle a trade payable

228 The bank accepts the instrument drawn upon it by its customer, and then sells it into a secondary market at a discount, including a commission, passing the proceeds to its client. The bank then pays the bill at face value.

Which description best describes this instrument?

- A A letter of credit
- B A forfaiting agreement
- C An acceptance credit
- D A commercial bill

229 Which of the following most appropriately describes forfaiting?

- A It is a method of providing medium-term export finance
- B It provides short-term finance for purchasing non-current assets which are denominated in a foreign currency
- C It provides long-term finance to importers
- D It is the forced surrender of a share due to the failure to make a payment on a partly paid share

SUBJECT F1: FINANCIAL REPORTING

230 Place THREE of the following options into the highlighted boxes in the table below to correctly show forms of short-term finance generally available to small entities.

Short-term government bonds
Interest bearing bank accounts
Trade payables
Negotiable instruments
Factoring
Invoice discounting

Forms of short-term finance

231 AL's customers all pay their accounts at the end of 30 days. To try and improve its cash flow, AL is considering offering all customers a 1.5% discount for payment within 14 days.

Calculate the implied annual (interest) cost to AL of offering the discount, using compound interest methodology and assuming a 365-day year.

_____ %. (Your answer should be rounded to one decimal place)

232 An entity's working capital policy is to hold as low level of cash and inventory as possible to save costs.

The above policy is an example of:

    A   an aggressive policy

    B   a conservative policy

    C   a short-term policy

    D   a moderate policy

233 BE has been offering 60-day payment terms to its customers, but now wants to improve its cash flow. BE is proposing to offer a 1.5% discount for payment within 20 days.

Assume a 365-day year and an invoice value of $1,000.

Calculate the effective annual interest rate that BE will incur for this action.

_____ %. (Your answer should be rounded to one decimal place)

234 The trade receivables ledger account for customer C shows the following entries:

		Debits	Credits
		$	$
Balance brought forward		0	
10 June X6	Invoice 201	345	
19 June X6	Invoice 225	520	
27 June X6	Invoice 241	150	
3 July X6	Receipt 1009 – Inv 201		200
10 July X6	Invoice 311	233	
4 August X6	Receipt 1122 – Inv 225		520
6 August X6	Invoice 392	197	
18 August X6	Invoice 420	231	
30 August X6	Receipt 1310 – Inv 311		233
7 September X6	Invoice 556	319	
21 September X6	Receipt 1501 – Inv 392		197
30 September X6	Balance	845	

Place FOUR of the following options into the highlighted boxes in the table below to correctly prepare an aged analysis showing the outstanding balance on a monthly basis for customer C at 30 September 20X6.

1,015	33	428	0
233	295	122	(325)
231	195	319	122

	Aged analysis
	$
June	
July	
August	
September	
	845

235 Which of the following would be LEAST likely to arise from the introduction of a Just-in-Time inventory ordering system?

    A   Lower inventory holding costs

    B   Less risk of inventory shortages

    C   More frequent deliveries

    D   Increased dependence on suppliers

236 Which of the following is LEAST relevant to the simple economic order quantity (EOQ) model for inventory?

  A   Safety stock

  B   Annual demand

  C   Holding costs

  D   Order costs

237 PB uses 2,500 units of component X per year. Its production director has calculated that the cost of placing and processing a purchase order for component X is $185, and the cost of holding one unit of component X for a year is $25.

What is the economic order quantity (EOQ) for component X and, assuming a 52-week year, what is the average frequency at which purchase orders should be placed?

	EOQ	Frequency of orders
A	136 units	3 weeks
B	136 units	6 weeks
C	192 units	4 weeks
D	192 units	5 weeks

238 Calculate the economic order quantity (EOQ) for the following item of inventory.

_____ units. (Your answer should be rounded up to the nearest unit)

- quantity required per year 32,000 items
- order costs are $15 per order
- inventory holding costs are estimated at 3% of inventory value per year
- each unit currently costs $40.

239 The economic order quantity formula includes the cost of placing an order. However, the Management Accountant is unsure which of the following items should be included in cost of placing an order.

Which THREE of the following would usually be regarded as part of the cost of placing an order?

  A   Administrative costs

  B   Postage

  C   Quality control cost

  D   Unit cost of products

  E   Storekeeper's salary

  F   Warehouse overheads

240 DS uses the Economic Order Quantity (EOQ) model. Demand for DS's product is 95,000 units per annum. Demand is evenly distributed throughout the year. The cost of placing an order is $15 and the cost of holding a unit of inventory for a year is $3.

Calculate how many orders DS should make in a year.

_____ orders. (Your answer should be rounded up to the nearest unit)

241 DF is a manufacturer of sports equipment that has recently won a major three-year contract to supply FF with a range of equipment. FF is a large company with over 100 sports shops.

The new contract is expected to double DF's existing total annual sales, but demand from FF will vary considerably from month to month.

The contract will mean a significant additional investment in current assets. In particular, the contract with FF will require orders to be delivered within two days. This delivery period gives DF insufficient time to manufacture items, therefore significant inventories need to be held at all times. Also, FF requires 90 days' credit from its suppliers. This will result in a significant additional investment in receivables by DF.

If DF borrows from its bank to finance current assets, either using a loan or an overdraft, it expects to be charged annual interest at 12%. Consequently, DF is considering offering a 3% cash discount to FF for settlement within 10 days rather than the normal 90 days.

Place FOUR of the following options into the highlighted boxes in the table below to correctly show which of the following would be factors, other than the rate of interest, which DF would need to consider before deciding on whether to offer a cash discount.

Borrowing on overdraft might be more risky
It is cheaper to finance the higher receivables by borrowing than it would be to offer the cash settlement discount
The cash settlement discount arrangement may be difficult to withdraw at a future time, if DF no longer wants to offer it
Other customers might demand the same settlement discount terms as FF
It is more expensive to finance the higher receivables by borrowing than it would be to offer the cash settlement discount
Borrowing on overdraft might be less risky
The cash discount will be more flexible and easier to cancel if DF no longer wants to offer it

Factors to consider for offering a discount

SUBJECT F1: FINANCIAL REPORTING

242 Calculate the annual equivalent rate of interest implicit in offering a 2% cash discount to for settlement of debts within 10 days rather than 40 days.

Assume a 365-day year and an invoice value of $100.

_____ %. (Your answer should be rounded up to two decimal places)

243 SCL is a wholesale supplier of building materials. It is experiencing severe short-term cash flow difficulties. Sales invoices are about $2 million per month. The usual credit period extended to customers is 60 days, but the average period being taken is 90 days. The overdraft rate is 9% per annum.

A factoring company has offered a full factoring agreement without recourse on a permanent basis. The factor will charge a fee of 2.5% on total invoicing and will provide an immediate advance of 80% of invoiced amounts at an annual interest rate of 10%. Settlement of the remaining 20% will be after 60 days. SCL should avoid $300,000 a year in the administration costs of running the receivables ledger if the factoring arrangement is taken up.

Calculate the annual net cost, in cash terms, of the proposed factoring agreement assuming that there are 360 days in a year.

$ _____. (Your answer should be rounded to the nearest $)

244 The trade receivables ledger account for customer X is as follows:

		Debits	Credits	Balance
01 July	Balance b/fwd			162
12 July	Invoice AC34	172		334
14 July	Invoice AC112	213		547
28 July	Invoice AC215	196		743
08 August	Receipt RK 116 (Balance + AC34)		334	409
21 August	Invoice AC420	330		739
03 September	Receipt RL162 (AC215)		196	543
12 September	Credit note CN92 (AC112)		53	490
23 September	Invoice AC615	116		606
25 September	Invoice AC690	204		810
05 October	Receipt RM223 (AC420)		330	480
16 October	Invoice AC913	233		713
25 October	Receipt RM360 (AC615)		116	597

Place the following options into the highlighted boxes in the table overleaf to correctly prepare an aged analysis showing the outstanding balance on a monthly basis for customer X at 31 October.

204	743	233	(4)
(213)	160	581	320
0	330	71	233

70

	Aged analysis
	$
July	
August	
September	
October	
	———
	597
	———

245 Complete the sentence below by placing one of the following options into the space.

An aged analysis of receivables allows an entity to _____. It makes it more obvious whether an increase/decrease in a balance is due to changed activity levels or a change in payment policy by a customer. This makes it easier for the company to assess whether it should carry on doing business, how it should _____ and whether it _____.

| should offer discounts |
| set credit limits |
| focus its collection efforts to enforce its credit terms |
| see the total amount owed by customers |
| needs to take any action in respect of large balances |
| chase debts |

246 BF manufactures a range of domestic appliances. Due to past delays in suppliers providing goods, BF has had to hold an inventory of raw materials, in order that the production could continue to operate smoothly. Due to recent improvements in supplier reliability, BF is re-examining its inventory holding policies and recalculating economic order quantities (EOQ).

- Item 'Z' costs BF $10.00 per unit.
- Expected annual production usage is 65,000 units.
- Procurement costs (cost of placing and processing one order) are $25.
- The cost of holding one unit for one year has been calculated as $3.

Calculate the EOQ for item 'Z'.

_____ units. (Your answer should be rounded to the nearest unit)

SUBJECT F1: FINANCIAL REPORTING

247 DF, a sports and fitness training equipment wholesaler, has prepared its forecast cash flow for the next six months and has calculated that it will need $2 million additional short-term finance in three months' time.

DF has an annual gross revenue of $240 million and achieves a gross margin of 50%. It currently has the following outstanding working capital balances:

- $16 million trade payables, typical payables days for this industry is 45 days
- $20 million trade receivables, typical receivable days for this industry is 30 days
- $25 million bank overdraft.

DF forecasts that it will be able to repay half the $2 million within three months and the balance within a further three months.

Which THREE of the following are possible sources of short-term funding available to DF?

A   Bank overdraft

B   Factoring of receivables

C   Increasing payables days

D   Reducing receivables days

E   Short-term loan

F   Invoice discounting

248 Place THREE of the following options into the highlighted boxes in the table below to show correctly forms of short-term investments generally available to small entities.

Short-term government bonds
Interest bearing bank accounts
Trade payables
Negotiable instruments
Factoring
Invoice discounting

Forms of short-term investments

249 Place the following options into the highlighted boxes in the table below to correctly show the advantages and disadvantages of using bank overdrafts and short-term bank loans.

Generally more expensive	Repayable on demand
Fixed finance cost	Repayment date known
Flexible	Less flexible
Generally cheaper	Variable finance cost

	Bank overdrafts	Bank loans
Advantage		
Advantage		
Disadvantage		
Disadvantage		

250 Which TWO of the following are indicators of overtrading?

- A A rapid decrease in current assets
- B A rapid increase in turnover
- C A rapid increase in liquidity ratios
- D A rapid decrease in turnover
- E A rapid increase in current assets

251 Which of the following does NOT influence the credit policy of an entity?

- A Demand for products
- B Profitability of products
- C Competitor terms
- D Risk of irrecoverable debts

252 Which of the following is an advantage of using a factoring agency for the collection of receivables?

- A Customers will not know the debt has been sold to a factor
- B Easy to change back to an internal debt collection system
- C Cheaper than an internal debt collection system
- D Savings on administration costs

253 Which of the following is an advantage of using an invoice discounting agency over a factoring agency?

- A Invoice discounting is cheaper than factoring
- B The debt collection is usually faster when using an invoice discounting agency
- C The entity retains control over debt collection
- D It is less risky than factoring

Section 2

ANSWERS TO OBJECTIVE TEST QUESTIONS

PRINCIPLES OF TAX

1   The competent jurisdiction is **the country whose tax laws apply to the entity**.

2   A taxable person is **the person or entity who is accountable for the tax payment**.

3   **A and B**

4   **D**

5   Tax evasion is **an illegal way of avoiding paying taxes**, i.e. not declaring income or claiming false expenses.

6   **C**

7   A direct tax is one that **is levied directly on the person who is intended to pay the tax**.

8   **D**

9   **A**
    Formal incidence

10 **C**

11 **D**

12 **A**
    A tax authority is unlikely to have the power of arrest. This power will usually be restricted to the police or other law enforcement officers.

SUBJECT F1: FINANCIAL REPORTING

13 A and D

The OECD's list of permanent establishments includes a place of management, a workshop and a quarry. A building site is only included if it lasts more than 12 months. Specifically excluded from the definition of permanent establishment are facilities used only for the purpose of storage, display or delivery of goods. A branch is considered as a permanent establishment not a subsidiary.

14 C

A = 17/75 = 22.7% tax paid on profits

B = 4.8/44 = 10.9% tax paid on profits

Therefore, the greater the profits, the greater the tax percentage, hence this is a progressive tax.

15 A, E and F

B, C and D are possibly results of setting deadlines because if tax is paid on time it is likely it will cost less to collect it, therefore easier to administer and it is possible payments will be more accurate if the return is done sooner rather than later. However, these three are not the main reasons for setting deadlines.

16 C

Equity

17 A, B and F

C is incorrect as although payments may be more accurate if the employer is using a software package to calculate the tax it is not necessary so. Self-assessment calculations should also be correctly calculated. D is incorrect as the employee has no cost of using the PAYE system and E is incorrect as this is a benefit to the employee and not the government.

18 From the revenue authority's point of view, a commodity is suitable for an excise duty to be imposed if:

Suitable for excise duties
There are few large producers/suppliers
Demand is inelastic with no close substitutes
Sales volumes are large

19 (i) & (ii)

20 A

Hypothecation is the means of devoting certain types of expenditure for certain things, e.g. Road tax is used for maintaining roads.

21 C

ANSWERS TO OBJECTIVE TEST QUESTIONS : SECTION 2

22   A and C

B, D and E are the same as income.

23   (ii) & (iv)

24   A

25   A

HD has the responsibility to pay the sales tax to the tax authorities and will have direct contact with them, therefore this is known as formal incidence.

26   B

27   B

28 $3,133

DB – Corporate income tax 20X6

	$
Profit before tax per accounts	33,950
Add back:	
Entertaining	600
Local government tax	950
Depreciation on buildings	1,600
Depreciation on plant and equipment	20,000
	57,100
Less: tax depreciation	
Building (70,000 × 4%)	(2,800)
Plant and equipment (W1)	(25,768)
Taxable profit	28,532

			Tax $
Taxable at 15%	(25,000 – 10,000) =	15,000	2,250
Taxable at 25%	(28,532 – 25,000) =	3,532	883
Corporate income tax 20X6			3,133

SUBJECT F1: FINANCIAL REPORTING

(W1)

	Plant and equipment $	New plant $	Total $
Cost	80,000		
20X5 tax depreciation @ 27%	(21,600)		
	58,400		
20X6 tax depreciation @ 27%	(15,768)		15,768
Cost		20,000	
20X6 first year allowance @ 50%		(10,000)	10,000
	42,632	10,000	25,768

29 D

	$
Accounting profit	860,000
Add depreciation	42,000
Add amortisation	15,000
	917,000
Less tax depreciation	(51,000)
Taxable profit	866,000
Tax @ 25%	216,500

30 D

31 D

32 Under the OECD model tax convention an entity will generally have residence for tax purposes in **the country of its effective management**.

33 B

34

Powers of the tax authority
Power to exchange information with tax authorities in other jurisdictions
Power to review and query filed returns

35 (ii) & (iii)

36 An example of an indirect tax would be excise tax.

ANSWERS TO OBJECTIVE TEST QUESTIONS : SECTION 2

37 (iii) & (iv)

38 Tax avoidance is **a legal way of avoiding taxes.** It is tax planning to arrange affairs, within the scope of the law, to minimise the tax liability.

39 C

Entities can use any rate for accounting depreciation, so to ensure that all entities are taxed equally the tax authority sets rates for tax depreciation for all entities. The tax depreciation rates then replace accounting depreciation in the tax computations and it can be greater or less depending on the tax rules in force in the country of residence.

40 D

41 $2,837

FB – Corporate income tax

	$
Profit for the year	29,800
Add back:	
Depreciation building	3,200
Depreciation plant and equipment	6,000
Depreciation furniture and fittings	5,000
Less: Accounting gain on disposal	(4,000)
	40,000
Less: Tax depreciation	
FYA – plant and equipment ($30,000 × 50%)	(15,000)
Buildings ($80,000 × 5%)	(4,000)
Disposal balancing allowance	(6,812)
(Proceeds $5,000 – TWDV $11,812)	
Taxable profit	14,188
Tax at 20%	2,837

42 D

Excise duties are placed on inelastic products not elastic.

43

Type of tax	Single stage	Multi-stage
Characteristic	Tax at one level of production	Tax at each level of production
Characteristic		This could be cascade tax
Characteristic		This could be VAT

SUBJECT F1: FINANCIAL REPORTING

44 A, C and D

B is incorrect because VAT will not be charged on all supplies, only taxable supplies and E is incorrect because VAT can only be recovered on purchases if the purchase is used to produce a taxable supply. F is incorrect as standard returns are made quarterly and not monthly.

45

Year	Taxable profits	Taxable gains
1	$ nil	$6,000
2	$ nil	$ nil
3	$ nil	$ nil
4	$60,000	$3,000

Year 1: No taxable trading profits and taxable capital gains of $6,000. $50,000 of the trading losses in Year 2 can be carried back and set off against the profit in Year 1, reducing the taxable trading profit to 0. The capital loss in Year 2 cannot be carried back to Year 1.

Year 2: No taxable trading profits or gains. Trading loss and capital loss in the year. Unrelieved trading losses of $40,000 and the unrelieved capital losses of $8,000 are carried forward to Year 3.

Year 3: No taxable trading profits or gains. Unrelieved trading losses of $40,000 are set against the trading profits of $30,000. The unrelieved trading loss is now $10,000 and is carried forward to Year 4. The unrelieved capital loss brought forward is set off against the capital gain in Year 3, leaving $3,000 of unrelieved capital losses to carry forward to Year 4.

Year 4: Taxable trading profits of $60,000 and taxable capital gains of $3,000. Taxable trading profits = $70,000 – $10,000 unrelieved losses brought forward. Taxable capital gains = $6,000 – $3,000 unrelieved losses brought forward.

46 C

Group loss relief allows members of the group to surrender their losses to any other member of the group. Consolidation of profits and losses does not apply to tax computations and so answer A is incorrect. Group loss relief is an option that can be taken by the group, and is not compulsory. Therefore answers B and D are incorrect.

47

Year	Corporate income tax due	Capital tax due
30 September 20X3	$40,000	$ nil
30 September 20X4	$ nil	$ nil
30 September 20X5	$6,000	$6,000

30 September 20X3   Trading profit $200,000 × 20% = $40,000

Capital loss c/f $100,000 so nil taxable

30 September 20X4   Trading loss c/f $120,000 so nil taxable

Capital loss of $100,000 b/f is c/f so nil taxable

30 September 20X5   Trading profit $150,000 – $120,000 = $30,000 × 20% = $6,000

Capital gain $130,000 – $100,000 = $30,000 × 20% = $6,000

ANSWERS TO OBJECTIVE TEST QUESTIONS : SECTION 2

48 **A and D**

Relief can be claimed earlier because if the surrendering entity keeps the loss for their own use it will be carried forward for many years. The group company may pay tax at a higher rate, therefore more tax can be saved by reducing the taxable profit.

49 **A**

	$
Disposal proceeds	1,200,000
Selling costs	(9,000)
Net proceeds	1,191,000
Cost	(600,000)
Additional costs	(5,000)
	586,000
Indexation (605,000 × 60%)	(363,000)
Taxable gain	223,000
Tax @ 25%	55,750

50 **$41,400**

		$
Disposal proceeds		1,250,000
Less: Costs of disposal		(2,000)
		1,248,000
Acquisition costs:		
Purchase cost	630,000	
Costs arising on purchase ($3,500 + $6,500)	10,000	
Renovation costs	100,000	
		(740,000)
Indexation – 50% × $740,000		(370,000)
Taxable gain		138,000
Tax @ 30%		41,400

SUBJECT F1: FINANCIAL REPORTING

51 **$42,625**

	$
Disposal proceeds	1,200,000
Costs to sell	(17,000)
Net proceeds	1,183,000
Cost	(650,000)
Duties	(25,000)
	508,000
Indexation (675,000 × 50%)	(337,500)
Taxable gain	170,500
Tax @ 25%	42,625

52 **$12,000**

	$
Disposal proceeds	450,000
Costs to sell	(15,000)
Net proceeds	435,000
Cost	(375,000)
Duties	(12,000)
Taxable gain	48,000
Tax @ 25%	12,000

53 **D**

The site of the 11 month construction contract is not a permanent establishment according to the OECD model because it is less 12 months.

54 **B**

An overseas branch is an extension of the main business activity and not treated as a separate entity for taxation purposes.

55 **C**

Withholding tax is a tax deducted at source before payment of interest or dividends.

ANSWERS TO OBJECTIVE TEST QUESTIONS : SECTION 2

56

Type of tax	Cascade tax	VAT
Characteristic	Multi-stage	Multi-stage
Characteristic	Tax at each level of production	Tax at each level of production
Characteristic	No refunds are provided by local government on purchase tax	Refunds are provided on purchase tax provided the purchases are used for a taxable supply

57 $29,000

		$
Disposal proceeds		1,000,000
Less: Costs of disposal		(6,000)
		994,000
Acquisition costs:		
Purchase cost	850,000	
Costs arising on purchase ($5,000 + $8,000)	13,000	
Clearing land costs	15,000	
		(878,000)
Taxable gain		116,000
Tax @ 25%		29,000

58   Under the OECD model an entity will have residence **in the country of effective management**.

59   **D**

Each of the other three factors can be taken into account in determining tax residence.

60   **C**

Effective management and control is the over-riding test under the OECD model tax convention.

61   **D**

The tax deducted at source from the dividend in the foreign country prior to distribution to EB is called the withholding tax.

62   **B**

Double tax relief does not prevent you from paying tax twice. For example, suppose that your company is based in Country A and has a subsidiary operating in Country B, and there is a double taxation agreement between the countries. If tax on profits in Country B is 10% and in Country A is 15%, your company would pay tax at 10% in Country B and tax at 15% in Country A on the subsidiary's profits. Double tax relief therefore mitigates tax – you don't have to pay 35% in tax (10% + 25%) – but you might still have to pay tax on the profits twice, once in each country.

63 C

The country of control overrides the others for residency.

64 D

65 A and B

66 D

67

Type of supply	Zero rated	Exempt
Characteristic	Entity must register for VAT purposes	Entity does not register for VAT purposes
Characteristic	VAT can be claimed back on purchases	VAT cannot be claimed back on purchases

68 A capital gain is **the profit made on the disposal of a chargeable asset**.

69 A capital tax is **the tax charged on the profit made on the disposal of a chargeable asset**.

70 A tax base represents **what is being taxed**.

71 $17,500

(4/12 × $75,000 × 20%) + (8/12 × $75,000 × 25%)

72 A, C and E

A tax base is something that is liable to tax, e.g. income or consumption of goods.

Tax bases regularly used by governments are:

- income – for example, income taxes and taxes on an entity's profits
- capital or wealth – for example, taxes on capital gains and taxes on inherited wealth
- consumption – for example, excise duties and sales taxes/VAT.

73 $22,500

	$
Accounting profit	95,000
Adjustments:	
Non-taxable income	(15,000)
Non-tax allowable expenditure	10,000
Taxable profits	90,000
Tax at 25%	22,500

ANSWERS TO OBJECTIVE TEST QUESTIONS : SECTION 2

74 Benefits in kind represent **non-cash benefits given to an employee as part of their remuneration package**.

75 **$37,250**

KQ – Corporate income tax

	$
Accounting profit	147,000
Adjustments:	
Add back: disallowed expenses (9,000 + 6,000)	15,000
Add back: accounting depreciation (180,000 + 50,000) × 15%	34,500
Less: tax depreciation (W1)	(47,500)
Taxable profits	149,000
Tax at 25%	37,250

(W1)

	$
Tax depreciation:	
First year allowance 50,000 × 50% =	25,000
Annual allowance (180,000 – 90,000 FYA 50% for 30/9/X1) × 25% =	22,500
Total tax depreciation	47,500

76 **A, B and D**

Excise Duty is a selective commodity tax, levied on certain types of goods. It is a unit tax based on the weight or size of the tax base. E.g. Petroleum products, tobacco products alcoholic drinks and motor vehicles.

From the revenue authority's point of view, the characteristics of commodities that make them most suitable for excise duty to be applied are:

- Few large producers
- Inelastic demand with no close substitutes
- Large sales volumes
- Easy to define products covered by the duty

SUBJECT F1: FINANCIAL REPORTING

77 **$200,250**

The accounting profit should be reported before recognising any dividends paid.

		$
Accounting profit		822,000
Add:	Entertaining expenses	32,000
	Donation to political party	50,000
Less:	Government grant income	(103,000)
		801,000
Tax @ 25%		200,250

78

	Tax avoidance	Tax evasion
Characteristic	A legal way of reducing your tax bill	An illegal way of reducing your tax bill
Characteristic	For example AB invests surplus income into tax-free securities to avoid paying tax on the interest	For example AB does not declare his income from his night security job

79 B

80 (ii) & (iii)

81 D

82 B

83 D

84 **$35,250**

	$	$
Disposal proceeds		210,000
Acquisition costs:		
Purchase cost	55,000	
Costs arising on purchase	5,000	
Indexation ($55,000 + $5,000) × 15%	9,000	
		(69,000)
Taxable gain		141,000
Tax @ 25%		35,250

… ANSWERS TO OBJECTIVE TEST QUESTIONS : SECTION 2

85 **B and D**

86 **B**

87 **$2,970**

	$
Disposal proceeds	80,000
Costs to sell	(2,000)
Net proceeds	78,000
Acquisition costs:	
Purchase cost	50,000
Import duties	8,000
Indexation ($50,000 + $8,000) × 14%	8,120
	(61,120)
Taxable gain	11,880
Tax @ 25%	2,970

88 **A**

	$
Disposal proceeds	110,000
Acquisition costs:	
Purchase cost	45,000
Costs arising on purchase	5,000
Indexation ($45,000 + $5,000) × 35%	17,500
	(67,500)
Taxable gain	42,500
Tax @ 25%	10,625

89 An indexation allowance **reduces a chargeable gain**.

90 **B**

A = 15/75 = 20% tax paid on profits

B = 8/40 = 20% tax paid on profits

Therefore, the regardless of the profits, the tax percentage remains the same, hence this is a proportionate tax.

91

	Transfer pricing
Characteristic	This results in transactions not taking place at 'arm's length' and profits being effected by the group members
Characteristic	This arises in group situations when either goods are sold inter-company or loans take place at a favourable price

THE REGULATORY ENVIRONMENT OF FINANCIAL REPORTING

92 An asset is **a present economic resource controlled by the entity as a result of past events**.

93 The objective of financial reporting is **to provide information about the reporting entity that is useful to users in making decisions relating to providing resources to the entity**.

94 B

Relevance is a fundamental qualitative characteristic, not an enhancing characteristic.

Prudence is considered when providing a faithful representation, which is another fundamental qualitative characteristic.

95 D

The IFRS Interpretations Committee interprets International Financial Reporting Standards and, after public consultation and reporting to the IASB, it issues an interpretation.

96 A

The IFRS Foundation is the supervisory body, and consists of trustees whose main responsibilities are governance issues and ensuring that sufficient funding is available.

97 C and E

98 The elements are assets, liabilities, income, **expenses** and **equity**.

99 B, D and E

100 The IASB's *Framework* identifies two methods of capital maintenance which are the **financial** concept and the **physical** concept.

101 The IASB's *Framework* identifies the underlying assumption as the **going concern** concept.

102 D

ANSWERS TO OBJECTIVE TEST QUESTIONS : SECTION 2

103 D

You should learn the IASB definitions of all the elements of the financial statements. B is the version of the definition of a liability before the recent revision to the conceptual framework. **Note:** References to 'outflow of economic benefits' has been replaced with 'transfer of economic resource'.

104 C

The IASB *Framework* states that materiality is a threshold or cut-off point for reporting information, but is not a qualitative characteristic that financial information must have to be useful.

105 Expenses are decreases in assets or increases in liabilities that result in **decreases** in equity, other than those relating to distributions to equity participants'

106 A

107 A and E

108 C

The IASB *Framework* defines equity as the residual interest in the assets of the enterprise after all the liabilities have been deducted from total assets. It is important to recognise this idea that equity is a balancing figure: Assets – Liabilities. Statements of financial position should be prepared with a view to measuring assets and liabilities in the best manner, and equity is the amount left over when liabilities are subtracted from assets.

109 D

110 D

E stands to make a gain if he manipulates the figures to get a better bonus, hence E is in a position of a self-interest threat.

111

Factors influencing accounting and disclosure
Social
Economic
Political

112 B

113 C

114

Functions of the IFRS Advisory Council
To give advice to the IASB on agenda decisions
To give advice to the IASB on the priorities in its work
To give any other advice to the IASB or the Trustees

115
The TWO fundamental qualitative characteristics are **relevance** and **faithful representation**.

116
D

117
A

118
(ii) & (iv)

119

	Adopting International Financial Reporting Standards (IFRS) as its local standards	Modelling local accounting standards on the IASB's IFRSs, but amending them to reflect local needs and conditions	Develop its own accounting standards with little or no reference to IFRSs
Advantage	Quick to implement	Standards should be more relevant to local needs and compliant with International Standards	Any standards developed will be specific to C's requirements
Disadvantage	Standards may not take into account any specific local traditions or variations	It will take longer to implement and requires an adequate level of expertise to exist within the country	It will not be quick to implement

120

The purpose of the Framework
Assist all parties to understand and interpret the Standards
Assist the IASB in the development of future IFRSs and in its review of existing IFRSs

ANSWERS TO OBJECTIVE TEST QUESTIONS : SECTION 2

121

Principle-based accounting standards	Prescriptive accounting standards
The standard would be applied using professional judgement	The standard would require a certain treatment to be used, regardless of the situation
Flexible	Less flexible
Standards should ensure the spirit of the regulations are adhered to	Standards more likely to lead to the letter of the law being followed rather than the spirit

122 Income is **increases in economic benefits during the accounting period in the form of inflows or enhancements of assets; or decreases of liabilities that result in increases in equity, other than those relating to combinations from equity participants**.

123 The Framework criteria states to be recognised in the financial statements, items must:

- meet the definitions of one of the elements of the financial statements
- provides relevant information regarding the particular element
- provides a faithful representation of the particular element

124 A and D

Self-interest – A professional accountant should not allow their own interests to override professional or business judgements. CX will be worried that her job may be lost if she does not comply with management's orders. As a result she may knowingly publish misstated information.

Intimidation – A professional accountant should not allow threats or intimidation to compromise their professional judgements. The management board are attempting to override CX's professional and business judgement. This would be deemed an intimidation threat.

125

	Dealing with an ethical dilemma
1	Gather evidence and document the problem
2	Report internally to immediate management
3	Report internally to higher management
4	Report externally
5	Remove herself from the situation

126 D

RS may be tempted to action the suggestions made by other employees simply to ensure they gained personally through the receipt of the bonus and the incentives. This would be a self-interest ethical threat.

There is nothing in the scenario that suggests RS relationship with the other employees is close enough to create a familiarity threat.

127

IFRS Foundation	International Accounting Standards Board (IASB)	IFRS Advisory Council	IFRS Interpretations Committee
Governance and fund raising	Responsibility for all technical matters including the preparation and publication of international financial reporting standards	Provides strategic advice to the IASB and informs the IASB of public views on major standard setting projects	Provides timely guidance on the application and interpretation of IFRSs

128 A, C and D

The ethical problem that XQ faces is that a professional accountant in business should prepare or present information fairly, honestly and in accordance with relevant professional standards so that the information will be understood in its context. A professional accountant is expected to act with integrity and objectivity and not allow any undue influence from others to override his or her professional judgement.

XQ is facing pressure from others to change the results and therefore break the CIMA Code.

XQ is being asked to misrepresent the facts of the actual situation which would be contrary to the CIMA Code's fundamental principles of integrity and objectivity. XQ would also be breaking the due care requirement of the CIMA Code.

129 C

He or she should start by gathering all relevant information so that he or she can be sure of the facts and decide if there really is an ethical problem. All steps taken should be fully documented.

Initially he or she should raise his concern internally, possibly with the team's manager or a trusted colleague.

If this is not a realistic option, for example because of the relationship of the manager and the team member that Ace is concerned about, he or she may have to consider escalating the issue and speak to the manager's boss, a board member or a non-executive director. If there is an internal whistle blowing procedure or internal grievance procedure he or she should use that.

130 C

131 D

132 (i) & (iii)

ANSWERS TO OBJECTIVE TEST QUESTIONS : SECTION 2

133

Fundamental	Enhancing
Relevance	Comparability
Faithful representation	Timeliness
	Understandability
	Verifiability

134 C

135 B

136 The purpose of corporate governance is to protect the **shareholders**.

137 Corporate governance is the means by which a company is **directed** and **controlled**.

138 D

139

Rules-based	Principle-based
Applied in the US	Applied in the UK
Instils the code into law	Comply with the code or explain why
Penalties for transgression	Adhere to the spirit rather than the letter of the code

FINANCIAL STATEMENTS

140 **$13,778**

The calculation is as follows:

	$000
Profit before tax	12,044
Add Depreciation	1,796
Loss on sale of tangible non-current assets	12
	13,852
Increase in inventories	(398)
Increase in receivables	(144)
Increase in payables	468
Cash generated from operations	13,778

141 $105,000

	$000
Balance at 30 September 20X4	180
Revaluation (30 – 10)	20
Disposal at CA (90 – 85)	(5)
Depreciation	(40)
	155
Balance at 30 September 20X5	(260)
Purchases	105

Disposal

	$000		$000
Cost	90	Bank	15
Profit	10	Dep'n (balance)	85
	100		100

142 A

	$
Accrued interest b/f	12,000
Interest payable per statement of profit or loss	41,000
Accrued interest c/f	(15,000)
Paid	38,000

143 B $360,000

	$000
Total opening balance	460
Add: interest for the year	460
	920
Less: Total closing balance	(560)
Tax paid during the period	360

The interest income from the statement of profit or loss would be used as part of the interest received calculation which, within the statement of cash flow, is shown separately from interest paid.

144 A

Interest payable

		B/f	133
Paid	98	Statement of profit or loss	122
C/f	157		
	255		255

145 A and E

146 A, C and E

147 $3,641

	$
Cost	100,000
Depreciation 31/3/X3	(25,000)
	75,000
Depreciation 31/3/X4	(18,750)
	56,250
Depreciation 31/3/X5	(14,063)
	42,188
Depreciation 31/3/X6	(10,547)
	31,641
Recoverable amount	(28,000)
Impairment loss	3,641

148 $580,000

	Land $000	Buildings $000	Total $000
Cost	120	200	
Accumulated depreciation to the revaluation date	–	(100)	
Carrying value at the revaluation date	120	100	220
Revalued amount	200	600	800
Credit to revaluation reserve			580

SUBJECT F1: FINANCIAL REPORTING

149 C

The four definitions might all seem similar, but property, plant and equipment are **tangible** assets, not any assets. IAS 16 states that a tangible asset should be held for **more than one accounting period** (rather than for more than 12 months) to qualify as property, plant and equipment.

150 $129,000

	$
Cost of basic machine	100,000
Special modifications made to basic design	15,000
Supplier's engineer's time installing and initial testing of machine	2,000
Concrete base	12,000
	129,000

We do not include the three year maintenance cost as this is not a one off cost and would be expensed to the statement of profit or loss.

JT can reclaim back VAT hence would not form part of the cost of non-current assets.

151 A

IAS 16 states that when the revaluation model is used, revaluations should be made with sufficient regularity to ensure that the carrying value of the assets remain close to fair value. IAS 16 also states that, if one item in a class of assets is revalued, all the assets in that class must be revalued.

152 A and D

			$
1 July 20X2	Cost		50,000
30 June 20X3	Carrying amount	80% × 50,000	40,000
30 June 20X4	Carrying amount	60% × 50,000	30,000

On 1 July 20X4 the asset is revalued from a carrying amount of $30,000 to a fair value of $60,000, establishing a revaluation reserve of $30,000. There are three years of useful life remaining.

		$
30 June 20X5	Carrying amount = ⅔ × 60,000	40,000
1 July 20X5	Disposal proceeds	35,000
Loss on disposal		(5,000)

There is a loss on disposal of $5,000, and the $30,000 revaluation reserve is transferred to retained earnings as a movement on reserves.

153 A

As the lining of the furnace was identified as a separate item in the accounting records, its replacement will be viewed as capital expenditure. The other three options all involve either replacing part of an asset or restoring it to its original condition.

ANSWERS TO OBJECTIVE TEST QUESTIONS : SECTION 2

154 **$5,250 p.a.**

	$
1.10.X2 purchase	21,000
Depreciation to 30.9.X5	
21,000/6 × 3	(10,500)
Balance 30.9.X5	10,500

The machine will be used for two more years, at which point it will be worthless. Assuming that production is still profitable with the increased depreciation charge, it should be written off over its remaining useful life, such that the charge recognised in the year to 30 September 20X6 should be $5,250 ($10,500 × ½).

155 **$66,500**

Workings:

	$
Cost 1/4/X1	100,000
$100,000/10 × 2 years	(20,000)
Carrying amount 31/03/X3	80,000
To revaluation reserve	15,000
Revaluation (1/4/X3)	95,000
Depreciation $95,000/8 years	(11,875)
B/f 1/4/X4	83,125
Depreciation $83,125/5 years	(16,625)
Carrying amount at 31/3/X5	66,500

156 **D**

The allocation of EW's administration costs would not be included as these costs are not directly incurred as a result of carrying out the construction.

157 **C**

The asset was previously revalued by $200,000, therefore when it is devalued by $250,000 the reserve is removed and the balance charged to the statement of profit or loss.

158 B

The plant is an item of property, plant and equipment and is capitalised at cost. This includes directly attributable costs of bringing the asset to its current condition and location. IAS 16 states that purchase price and any decommissioning costs are part of the directly attributable costs and should be capitalised.

The amount to include in the cost of the asset for decommissioning costs is the present value of the expected future decommissioning costs. The present value is calculated by multiplying the expected future cost by a discount factor, which in this case is the discount factor for Year 5 (20X9) at 12%. $4,000,000 × 0.567 = $2.268 million.

The asset is depreciated on a straight-line basis over five years.

	$000
Cost of the plant	10,000
Decommissioning cost	2,268
Depreciation charge ($12.268 million/5 years)	(2,454)
Carrying amount	9,814

159 A and E

	Land $ million	Buildings $ million	Total $ million
At 30 June 20X5			
Carrying amount	1.00	4.80	5.80
Building depreciation = $5 million/50 years = $100,000 per year			
Revalued amount	1.24	5.76	7.00
Transfer to revaluation reserve			1.20
At 30 June 20X7			
Carrying amount	1.24	5.52	6.76
Building depreciation = $5.76 million/48 years = $120,000 per year			
Disposal value			6.80
Gain on disposal			0.04

The gain on disposal is $40,000. The $1.2 million balance on the revaluation reserve is transferred from the revaluation reserve to retained earnings in the SOCIE but is not reported through the statement of profit or loss for the year.

… ANSWERS TO OBJECTIVE TEST QUESTIONS : SECTION 2

160 $8,912

	$
Carrying amount at the time of the impairment review	38,912
($76,000 × 80% × 80% × 80%)	
Revised carrying amount after impairment review	30,000
Impairment (charge in the statement of profit or loss)	8,912

Note: The revised carrying amount (recoverable amount), is the higher of value in use $30,000 or fair value less costs to sell $27,000.

161 B $80,000

An asset should be valued at the lower of carrying amount and recoverable amount. Recoverable amount is the higher of (a) fair value less costs to sell and (b) value in use.

	A	B	C
Carrying amount	200	300	240
Recoverable amount	240	260	200
Impairment loss	nil	40	40

80

162 C

The recoverable amount of an asset is the higher of (a) fair value less costs to sell ($18,000) and (b) value in use ($22,000).

163 Property, plant and equipment note 31 December 20X5

	Land	Buildings	Plant and machinery	Under construction	Total
Cost/valuation	$000	$000	$000	$000	$000
Balance at 1 January 20X5	2,743	3,177	1,538	53	7,511
Revaluation of assets	375	–	–	0	375
Disposal of assets	–	–	(125)	–	(125)
Transfers	–	–	350	(350)	0
Additions	402	526	890	297	2,115
Balance at 31 December 20X5	3,520	3,703	2,653	0	9,876
Depreciation					
Balance at 1 January 20X5	–	612	671	–	1,283
Disposal of assets	–	–	(111)	–	(111)
Depreciation for the year	–	75	212	–	287
Balance at 31 December 20X5	0	687	772	0	1,459
Carrying amount 31 December 20X5	3,520	3,016	1,881	0	8,417
Carrying amount 31 December 20X4	2,743	2,565	867	53	6,228

164 $55,800

	Cost	Recoverable amount (Net Realisable Value)	Lower of cost and recoverable amount
Item 1	$24,000	See note 1	$24,000
Item 2	$33,600	$31,800 (note 2)	$31,800
			$55,800

Notes:

1. The recoverable amount is not known, but it must be above cost because the contract is expected to produce a high profit margin. The subsequent fall in the cost price to $20,000 is irrelevant for the inventory valuation.

2. The recoverable amount is $36,000 minus 50% of $8,400.

165 B, D and E

IAS 2 states that:

(a) selling costs cannot be included in inventory cost, therefore A cannot be included

(b) general overheads cannot be included C

(c) overhead costs should be added to inventory cost on the basis of normal capacity of the production facilities, therefore F cannot be included in cost

(d) the cost of factory management and administration can be included, so that item D can be included in inventory values.

ANSWERS TO OBJECTIVE TEST QUESTIONS : SECTION 2

166 D

The fire is an example of a non-adjusting event as it arose after the reporting date and does not provide evidence of a condition that existed at the reporting date.

167 C

The warehouse fire is an adjusting event as it occurred before the reporting date. Settlement of the insurance claim should therefore be included in the financial statements. The other events are non-adjusting as they occurred after the reporting date and do not provide evidence of conditions existing at the reporting date.

168 C and E

The share issue takes place after the reporting date is not an adjusting event. Plans to acquire another entity after the reporting date are not adjusting events.

169 B

170 D and E

Dividends declared after the reporting date but before the accounts are signed are not provided for but should be disclosed by way of note.

The dividend is shown as a deduction in the statement of changes in equity for the year in which it is actually paid.

171

Adjusting events	Non-adjusting events
One month after the reporting date a court determined a case against XS and awarded damages of $50,000 to one of XS's customers. XS had expected to lose the case and had set up a provision of $30,000 at the reporting date	A month after the reporting date XS's directors decided to cease production of one of its three product lines and to close the production facility
One month after the year end XS's main customer goes into liquidation owing XS a substantial amount of money	A dispute with workers caused all production to cease six weeks after the reporting date
XS discovers a material error in the closing inventory value one month after the reporting date	Three weeks after the reporting date a fire destroyed XS's main warehouse facility and most of its inventory

172 A

173 B and D

Expenses are analysed into cost of sales, distribution costs and administrative expenses.

174 C

Both items must be shown on the face of the statement of profit or loss. Other items to include in the statement of profit or loss include revenue, the tax expense and the profit or loss for the period (IAS 1).

175 A

IAS 1 states that the financial statements must be prepared on a going concern basis, unless management intends to liquidate the entity or to cease trading, or has no realistic alternative but to do so. When the financial statements are not prepared on a going concern basis, this fact must be disclosed. It is not therefore a requirement of IAS 1 that a note should state that the accounts are prepared on a going concern basis. (However, there might be a similar requirement, for example in a corporate governance code, that the directors should state in the annual report and accounts that the entity is a going concern.)

176 B and D

Revenue and finance costs must be shown on the face of the statement of profit or loss.

177 A

A revaluation of a non-current asset is not reported through the statement of profit or loss, but as an adjustment to the equity reserves (revaluation reserve account). The revaluation will therefore affect the statement of financial position and the statement of changes in equity, but not the statement of profit or loss. A revaluation is not a cash flow transaction, and so would not appear in the statement of cash flows.

178 C and D

At the date when an asset meets the criteria as an asset held for sale it should be shown separately on the statement of financial position and depreciation should cease.

179 A and D

According to CIMA's Code of ethics for professional accountants the finance director is in a position where he or she may be compromising his or her integrity and objectivity.

Integrity – This principle imposes an obligation to be truthful and honest on the accountant. A professional accountant should not be associated with reports and other information where she/he believes that the information contains misleading statements. This seems to be the case with the revised treatment of the property, the finance director believes that the revised financial statements will not follow IFRS 5 and may not show a true and fair view of the situation.

Objectivity – A professional accountant should not allow conflict of interest or undue influence of others to override professional or business judgements or to compromise her/his professional judgements. The management board is overriding the finance directors' professional and business judgement as it is imposing its business judgement over the professional accountant's.

ANSWERS TO OBJECTIVE TEST QUESTIONS : SECTION 2

180 B

The earthquake occurred after the end of the accounting period. Assets and liabilities at 31 August 20X9 were not affected. The earthquake is indicative of conditions that arose after the reporting period and does not give any further evidence in relation to assets and liabilities in existence at the reporting date. Therefore according to IAS 10 *Events after the Reporting Period* it will be classified as a non-adjusting event after the reporting period. The cost of the repairs will be charged to the Statement of profit or loss and other comprehensive income in the period when it is incurred. Due to the impact on MN, i.e. closure and loss of earnings for 6 months, the earthquake and an estimate of its effect will need to be disclosed by way of a note in MN's financial statements for the year ended 31 August 20X9.

181

Treatment of the asset held for sale
The assets have met the criteria of an asset held for sale
The assets should be shown separately as assets held for sale in the statement of financial position
The assets should be valued at $398,000
Impairment of $45,000 should be treated as an expense to the statement of profit or loss

EK can treat the sale of its asset as a held for sale asset as defined by IFRS 5 *Non-current Assets Held for Sale and Discontinued Operations* as it is held for sale. There is a plan to dispose of the asset, such that the economic value of the asset will be realised by selling, rather than continuing to use.

The assets should be recognised at the lower of:

- the value under normal accounting standards, i.e. $443,000
- the value on sale, being the fair value less the costs of sale, i.e. $423,000 less $25,000.

Therefore, EK should value the asset at $398,000.

This results in an impairment loss of $45,000 ($443,000 – $398,000), which should be recognised as an expense to the statement of profit or loss.

Once this valuation exercise has been performed, no depreciation or amortisation should be recognised.

182 $170

Non-current assets – PPE			
	$million		$million
Bfwd	645	Depn	120
		Disposal (CA)	60
Additions	170	Cfwd	635
	815		815

183 DV will **reduce the revaluation reserve** for the impact of the revaluation of the building on 31 August 20X6.

Workings	$
1.9.W6 Cost	200,000
Useful life	20
At first revaluation – 31.8.X1 – CA (200,000 × 15/20)	150,000
Revaluation gain	30,000
Valuation carried forward	180,000
At second revaluation – 31.8.X6 – CA (180,000 × 10/15)	120,000
Revaluation (loss)	(20,000)
Revaluation	100,000

The impairment is less than the revaluation reserve of $30,000, so the impairment is debited against the revaluation reserve, leaving a balance on that reserve of $10,000.

184 The answer is **$7,500 impairment**.

Building B	$
1.9.W6 Cost	120,000
Useful economic life	15
At first revaluation – 31.8.X1 – CV	120,000 × 10/15 = 80,000
Revaluation gain/(loss)	(5,000)
Valuation carried forward	75,000
At second revaluation – 31.8.X6 – CV	75,000 × 5/10 = 37,500
Revaluation gain/(loss)	(7,500)
Revaluation	30,000

The impairment on B of $7,500 goes to the statement of profit or loss, as there is no revaluation reserve in respect of that building.

185 **$72,000**

Proceeds from share issue = (460 + 82 – 400 – 70)

186 **C**

The inflow and outflow of the loans should be shown separately on the statement of cash flows.

Long term borrowings

	$000		$000
Payments	25	B/fwd	105
C/fwd	129	**Additions**	49
	154		154

ANSWERS TO OBJECTIVE TEST QUESTIONS : SECTION 2

187 B

Hotel G should be revalued to $650,000 and Hotel H to $820,000 from 1 January 20X4. The transfer to the revaluation reserve for Hotels G and H should be the difference between their carrying amount at 1 January 20X4 (before the revaluation) and their revalued amount. The carrying amount of the hotels is their cost less accumulated depreciation to 1 January 20X4. For Hotel G this was $346,000 ($650,000 – $304,000) and for Hotel H this was $126,000 ($820,000 – $694,000). This is a total of $472,000.

The reduction in value of Hotel K of $110,000 is not charged against this reserve. It is an impairment which is expensed.

188 An asset held for sale is an asset which is available for **immediate** sale in its present condition, and the sale is **highly probable**. This could be proven by meeting certain conditions, two of which are that there is an **active programme** to locate a buyer and that the asset is being actively marketed at a **reasonable** price.

189 A, C and D

190 C

The machine must be valued at the lower of carrying amount ($250,000) and recoverable amount ($230,000), i.e. $230,000. Recoverable amount is the higher of fair value less costs to sell ($230,000) and value in use ($150,000).

Working:

	$
Cost	500,000
Accumulated depreciation (500,000 × 5/10)	(250,000)
Carrying amount	250,000

The impairment loss of $20,000 ($250,000 – $230,000) must be charged to the statement of profit or loss in the year ended 30 September 20X5.

191 B

Building

	$
Cost	1,000,000
Y/e 30/9/X3 – Depreciation (1,000,000/20)	(50,000)
Y/e 30/9/X4 – Depreciation (1,000,000/20)	(50,000)
Carrying amount	900,000
Revaluation	1,800,000
Credit to revaluation reserve	900,000

192 $100,000

Depreciation will be based on the revalued figure: $1,800,000/18 years.

193 C

Following the revaluation, depreciation must be calculated on the revalued figure. There seems to have been no change to the estimate of the building's life, so 18 years of life remain.

Y/e 30/9/X5	$
Valuation b/f	1,800,000
Depreciation (1,800,000/18)	(100,000)
Carrying amount	1,700,000
Revaluation	1,500,000
Debit to revaluation reserve	200,000

As the building had previously been revalued upwards, the impairment loss can be debited to the revaluation reserve rather than being charged to the statement of profit or loss.

194 $88,235

Future depreciation will be based on the revalued figure: $1,500,000/17 years = $88,235 p.a.

195 $15,949

Lease liability = present value of lease rentals for 4 years discounted using rate implicit with the lease of 9%.

$70,000 × 3.240 = $226,800

Subsequent treatment – add finance cost less rental repayments

Year	Bal b/f	Interest at 9%	Paid	Bal c/f
	$	$	$	$
20X1	226,800	20,412	(70,000)	177,212
20X2	177,212	**15,949**	(70,000)	123,161

196 $56,250

	$
Total lease payments (9 × $125,000)	1,125,000
Lease term	/10 years
Annual charge to profit or loss	112,500

Charge in year ended 31 December 20X1 = 6/12 × 112,500 = $56,250

ANSWERS TO OBJECTIVE TEST QUESTIONS : SECTION 2

197 A

Initial value of liability = present value of lease rentals for 5 years discounted using rate implicit with the lease 7%

$110,000 × 4.100 = $451,000

Year	Bal b/f $	Interest at 7% $	Paid $	Bal c/f $
20X1	451,000	31,570	(110,000)	372,570
20X2	372,570	26,080	(110,000)	**288,650**

Non-current liability = amount outstanding after next year's payment

Direct costs would be capitalised as part of the right-of-use asset, not the lease liability

198 C

Depreciation of leased plant $68,000 ($340,000/5 years)

Finance cost $25,000 (($340,000 – $90,000) × 10%)

Rental of equipment $13,500 ($18,000 × $^9/_{12}$)

Total $106,500.

199 B

Year end	B/f $	Interest 7% $	Payment $	c/f $
31 October 20X3	45,000	3,150	(10,975)	37,175
31 October 20X4	37,175	2,602	(10,975)	28,802

The figure to the right of the payment in the next year is the non-current liability. Once 20X4's payment has been made, $28,802 will still be owed, making this the non-current liability. The current liability will be the difference between the total liability of $37,175 and the non-current liability of $28,802, which is $8,373.

If you selected C, you chose the total year-end liability rather than the non-current liability. If you selected A, you deducted the payment of $10,975 from the total. If you selected D you recorded the payment in advance and chose the year end liability rather than the non-current liability.

200 D

Assets permitted to be exempted from recognition are low-value assets and those with a lease term of 12 months or less. The use of the asset is irrelevant, and, although IFRS 16 *Leases* does not define low-value, it is the cost when new that is considered rather than current fair value.

SUBJECT F1: FINANCIAL REPORTING

201 A

Initial value of lease liability is the present value of lease payments, $86,240.

	Balance b/f	Payment	Subtotal	Interest @ 8%	Balance c/f
20X3	86,240	(20,000)	66,240	5,299	71,539
20X4	71,539	(20,000)	51,539	4,123*	55,662
20X5	55,662	(20,000)*	35,662*		

The non-current liability at 20X4 is the figure to the right of the payment in 20X5, $35,662. The current liability is the total liability of $55,662 less the non-current liability of $35,662, which is $20,000.

The finance cost is the figure in the interest column for 20X4, $4,123.

If you chose B you have done the entries for year one. If you chose C or D, you have recorded the payments in arrears, not in advance.

202 C

The transfer of ownership at the end of the lease indicates that Pigeon will have use of the asset for its entire life, and therefore 7 years is the appropriate depreciation period. Potential transactions at market rate would be ignored as they do not confer any benefit on Pigeon, and Pigeon's depreciation policy for purchased assets is irrelevant.

203 $58,000

The asset would initially be capitalised at $87,000. This is then depreciated over six years, being the shorter of the useful life and the lease term (including any secondary period).

This would give a depreciation expense of $14,500 a year. After two years, accumulated depreciation would be $29,000 and therefore the carrying amount would be $58,000.

204 B

Year end	b/f	Interest @ 10%	Payment	c/f
	$000	$000	$000	$000
30 September 20X4	23,000	2,300	(6,000)	19,300
30 September 20X5	19,300	1,930	(6,000)	15,230

Current liability at 30 September 20X4 = 19,300,000 − 15,230,000 = $4,070,000

205 D

The value recognised in respect of the lease payments will be the present value of future lease payments rather than the total value.

ANSWERS TO OBJECTIVE TEST QUESTIONS : SECTION 2

MANAGING CASH AND WORKING CAPITAL

206 (ii) & (iii)

Businesses that regularly fail to pay their suppliers on time may find it difficult to obtain future credit.

207 C

A conservative working capital policy would hold higher levels of working capital creating a longer working capital cycle.

Options A and B describe aggressive policy characteristics. D describes moderate policy characteristics.

208 $755,760

		Cash received $
April sales	20% × $780,000	156,000
March sales	80% × 0.98 × $770,000 × 60%	362,208
February sales	80% × 0.98 × $760,000 × 30%	178,752
January sales	80% × 0.98 × $750,000 × 10%	58,800
		755,760

209 $4,800

	Current assets $	Current liabilities $
Credit purchase:		
Inventory	+ 18,000	
Trade payables		+ 18,000
Credit sale:		
Trade receivables	+ 24,000	
Inventory (24,000 × 100/125)	– 19,200	

Working capital will increase by $4,800, as a result of the credit sale.

210 $252,000

	$
Budgeted sales	240,000
Expected decrease in receivables	12,000
	252,000

The reduction in receivables means that the entity will expect to receive more cash next month than the total of its credit sales for the month. Changes in inventory levels have no effect on expected cash receipts.

211 47 days

Receivables

	$		$
B/f	68,000	Returns	2,500
Sales	250,000	Cash	252,100
		Irrecoverable debts	
		(68,000 × 0.05)	3,400
		C/f	60,000
	318,000		318,000

Receivable days = 64/495 × 365 = 47.19 days, round down to 47 days

Average receivables = (68 + 60)/2 = $64,000

(**Note:** That the estimated sales cover a period of only six months, so the annual sales figure is $495,000 (2 × (250,000 – 2,500))

212 B

Working capital cycle		Days
Inventory	(8/30) × 365	97.3
Trade receivables	(4/40) × 365	36.5
Trade payables	(3/15) × 365	(73.0)
Cash conversion cycle		60.8

Note: The annual cost of purchases would be useful for measuring the inventory turnover period for raw materials. Since the question does not state whether inventory is mainly raw materials, work-in-progress or finished goods, it is probably appropriate to use the annual cost of sales to measure the average inventory turnover time. However, it is probably reasonable to assume that most trade payables relate to purchases of raw materials, and the annual purchases figure has therefore been used to calculate the payment cycle for trade payables.

ANSWERS TO OBJECTIVE TEST QUESTIONS : SECTION 2

213 C

Average receivables = ($10 million + $12 million)/2 = $11 million

Average trade-related receivables = 90% × $11 million = $9.9 million

Annual sales on credit = $95 million

Average collection period = (9.9 million/95 million) × 365 days = 38 days

214 B

	$
Balance b/fwd	22,000
Credit sales	290,510
	312,510
Less: Balance c/fwd ($290,510 × 49/365)	(39,000)
Receipts	273,510

215 $345,000

	$
Purchases on credit	360,000
Increase in trade payables	(15,000)
Therefore payments to suppliers	345,000

216 C

($82,000 − 12,250) × 97% = $67,657

217 $345,379

Trade payable days = Payable/credit purchases × 365

50 = (Payables/351,534) × 365

Payables = 50/365 × 351,534

Payables = $48,155

	$
Owed to credit suppliers at 1 November 20X6	42,000
Purchase on credit	351,534
Less: Amounts owed to credit suppliers at 31 October 20X7 50/365 × 350,000	(48,155)
Amount paid to credit suppliers during the year to 31 October 20X7	**345,379**

218 **88 days**

Trade receivable days = 290/2,400 × 365 = 44.1 days

Inventory days (assuming that inventories are finished goods) = 360/1,400 × 365 = 93.9 days

Trade payable days = 190/1,400 × 365 = 49.6 days

Working capital cycle = Inventory days + Receivable days – Payable days

= 93.9 + 44.1 – 49.6 = 88.4 days, round down to 88 days

219 **$19,800**

Sales in	Total sales $	Cash sales $	Credit sales $	Received in May	$
April	20,000	8,000	12,000	(97% × 12,000)	11,640
May	20,400	8,160	12,240		8,160
					19,800

220 **B**

Overtrading is associated with fast-growing companies that have insufficient long-term capital, and rely on short-term liabilities to finance their growth. The finance is largely provided by suppliers (trade payables) and a bank overdraft. As a result, there is an increasing bank overdraft (higher borrowing) and very low or even negative working capital. A typical overtrading enterprise is experiencing rapid growth and rising sales. Although it should be profitable, its problem will be a shortage of cash and liquidity. Cash balances will be not be rising, since the overdraft is increasing.

221 An aged trade creditor's analysis (aged trade payables analysis) **is a breakdown of trade payables according to length of time elapsing since the purchase was made**.

An aged analysis for trade payables is an analysis of unpaid invoices from suppliers according to the length of time since the issue of the invoice. It is not a list (therefore answer A and answer B are incorrect), but a table. A spreadsheet might be used to construct the analysis. The analysis can be used to decide which suppliers should be paid, and how much.

An aged analysis for trade receivables is similar, except that it relates to unpaid invoices sent to credit customers. This analysis is used to decide which customers to 'chase' for payment.

222 **C**

The equivalent annual return offered by supplier P is:

$(100/99)^{12} - 1 = 12.82\%$

This is below the minimum required rate of return of 12.85% and should not be accepted.

The equivalent annual return offered by supplier Q is:

$(100/98)^{12/2} - 1 = 12.89\%$

This is just above the minimum required rate of return of 12.85% and therefore should be accepted.

ANSWERS TO OBJECTIVE TEST QUESTIONS : SECTION 2

223 27.86%

Annual rate of interest = $(100/98)^{(365/30 - 0)} - 1$

= 0.2786 or 27.86%

224 A, C and E

225 Invoice discounting normally involves **selling an individual invoice for cash to a factor organisation at a discount**.

Invoice discounting is a method of obtaining short-term funds. Specific invoices are 'sold' to a finance organisation, typically a factor, which provides finance up to a proportion (about 70%) of the value of the invoice. The invoice discounter is repaid with interest out of the money from the invoice payment, when it is eventually paid.

226 D

If $1 million is invested for one year at 7%, the value of the investment will be $1,000,000 × 1.07 = $1,070,000 after one year.

If $1 million is invested for three months at 6.5% per year and then for nine months at 7.5% per year, this means that the interest for the first three months will be 6.5% × 3/12 = 1.625%, and the interest for the next nine months will be 7.5% × 9/12 = 5.625%. The value of the investment after one year will therefore be:

$1,000,000 × 1.01625 × 1.05625 = $1,073,414.

This is $3,414 more than the income that would be obtained by investing at 7% for the full year. However, there is a risk that interest rates will not rise during the first three months, and XYZ will not be able to invest at 7.5% for the nine months, but only at a lower rate.

227 A

The customer cannot be asked for immediate payment once a bill of exchange has been accepted.

228 C

The instrument is a bill of exchange drawn on the bank. This is often called a bank bill (as distinct from a commercial bill, which is a bill drawn on a non-bank company). A bill drawn on a bank under a short-term financing arrangement is also known as an acceptance credit.

229 A

Forfaiting is a method of obtaining medium-term export finance, involving the issue of promissory notes by the importer/buyer, which the exporter is able to sell to a forfaiting bank at a discount to obtain finance. Promissory notes are promises to pay a specified amount of money at a specified future date. The importer's promissory notes have settlement dates spread over a number of years, often the expected useful economic life of the imported items. The importer is therefore able to pay for the imported goods over a period of several years, whilst the exporter can obtain immediate payment by selling the promissory notes.

230

Forms of short-term finance
Trade payables
Factoring
Invoice discounting

The other items are forms of short-term investments.

231 41.2%

AL offers 1.5% interest for 16 days

$(100/98.5)^{(365/16)} - 1 =$

$= 41.2\%$

232 A

233 14.8%

Annual cost $= (100/98.5)^{(365/(60-20))} - 1$

$= (100/98.5)^{9.125} - 1$

$= 14.8\%$

234

	Aged analysis
	$
June	295
July	0
August	231
September	319
	———
	845
	———

Workings:

	$
June debts: 345 + 520 + 150 – 200 – 520	295
July debts: 233 – 233	0
Augusts debts: 197 + 231 – 197	231
September debts: 319	319
	———
	845
	———

ANSWERS TO OBJECTIVE TEST QUESTIONS : SECTION 2

235 B

With JIT purchasing, the objective is to receive deliveries exactly at the time required, so that the ideal inventory level is always 0. Therefore inventory holding costs should be lower. There will be an increased dependence on suppliers to deliver exactly on time, but there will be a risk (probably an increased risk) of inventory shortages due to failure by suppliers to deliver on time. However, since purchases will be made to meet demand requirements, there are likely to be much more frequent deliveries.

236 A

The simple EOQ model formula is:

$$EOQ = \sqrt{\frac{2cd}{h}}$$

Where: d = annual demand

h = cost of holding one unit for one year

c = cost of placing order

237 C

$$EOQ = \sqrt{\frac{2C_o D}{C_h}} = \sqrt{\frac{2 \times \$185 \times 2,500}{\$25}}$$

$$= \sqrt{37,000}$$

= 192 units

Each week $\frac{2,500}{52}$ = 48 units are required.

Therefore each order of 192 units will last $\frac{192}{48}$ = 4 weeks.

238 895 units

$$\sqrt{\frac{2 \times \$15 \times 32,000}{\$1.2}} = \sqrt{800,000} = 894.43 \text{ units} = \text{rounded to 895 units}$$

239 A, B and C

The cost of placing an order under the EOQ formula includes administrative costs, postage and quality control costs.

240 98 orders

$$Q = \sqrt{\frac{2C_o D}{C_h}}$$

$$\sqrt{\frac{2 \times 15 \times 95,000}{3}} = 974.68$$

95,000/975 = 97.4.

241

Factors to consider for offering a discount
Borrowing on overdraft might be more risky
It is cheaper to finance the higher receivables by borrowing than it would be to offer the cash settlement discount
Other customers might demand the same settlement discount terms as FF
The cash settlement discount arrangement may be difficult to withdraw at a future time, if DF no longer wants to offer it

1. The bank would charge annual interest of 12% which is less than the rate above. This means that it is cheaper to finance the higher receivables by borrowing than it would be to offer the cash settlement discount.

2. If DF borrows on overdraft from a bank, there is a risk that the bank might withdraw or reduce the overdraft facility without notice. Borrowing on overdraft might therefore be more risky.

3. Other customers might demand the same settlement discount terms as FF.

4. Once it has been established, the cash settlement discount arrangement may be difficult to withdraw at a future time, if DF no longer wants to offer it.

242 27.86%

Taking the discount is equivalent to receiving interest at a rate of 27.86%. Therefore if DN needs to increase its overdraft to make the payment, it is beneficial to do so as long as the interest rate charged is less than 27.86%.

Alternatively, it would be beneficial for DN to use any surplus cash in its current account or cash in any short-term investments yielding less than 27.86%.

Workings:

If DN pays $98 on day 10 instead of day 40, it will need to borrow $98 for 30 days.

The effective annual interest rate is:

$$\frac{365}{30} = 12.1667\%$$

$$1 + r = \left(\frac{100}{98}\right)^{12.1667}$$

$1 + r = 1.2786$

$r = 0.2786$ or 27.86%

ANSWERS TO OBJECTIVE TEST QUESTIONS : SECTION 2

243 $152,000

Annual sales $2 million × 12 = £24 million.

			$
Factor's annual fee	(2.5% × $24 million)		(600,000)
Saving in administration costs			300,000
		$	
Current average receivables	($24 million × 90/360)	6,000,000	
Receivables with the factor	(0.20 × $24m × 60/360)	800,000	
Reduction in average receivables		5,200,000	
Savings in interest at 9%			468,000
Factor finance interest	((0.80 × $24m × 60/360 × 10%)		(320,000)
Net annual cost			(152,000)

244

	Aged analysis
	$
July	160
August	0
September	204
October	233
	597

July = AC212 $192 – CN92 $53 = $160

September = AC690

October = AC913

245 An aged analysis of receivables allows an entity to **focus its collection efforts to enforce its credit terms**. It makes it more obvious whether an increase/decrease in a balance is due to changed activity levels or a change in payment policy by a customer. This makes it easier for the company to assess whether it should carry on doing business, how it should **set credit limits** and whether it **needs to take any action in respect of large balances**.

246 1,041 units

$$EOQ = \sqrt{\frac{2cd}{h}}$$

Where d = annual demand
  h = cost of holding one unit for one year
  c = cost of placing order

Therefore: $\sqrt{\frac{2 \times 25 \times 65,000}{3}} = 1,041$

SUBJECT F1: FINANCIAL REPORTING

247 **B, E and F**

DF could obtain short-term finance from any of the following sources:

- by increasing the overdraft, however, **this is unlikely** as the overdraft is already quite high
- by taking out a short-term loan
- by taking additional credit from suppliers

    DF currently has trade payable days outstanding of 49 days (16/120 × 365). An increase of $2 million to $18 million would be 55 days (18/120 × 365), this needs to be viewed against the credit period offered by the suppliers. As the typical payables days are 45, the increase would **probably not be acceptable** and could cause problems obtaining future credit.

- by improving the receivables collection period:

    DF's trade receivables collection period is currently 30 days (20/240 × 365), which is quite low and in line with the industry average. **So this is unlikely to be a viable option** as it would involve reducing the trade receivables collection period to 27 days (18/240 × 365).

- by factoring or invoice discounting.

248

Forms of short-term investments
Negotiable instruments
Short-term government bonds
Interest bearing bank accounts

The other items are types of short-term finance.

249

	Bank overdrafts	Bank loans
Advantage	Flexible	Fixed finance cost
Advantage	Generally cheaper	Repayment date known
Disadvantage	Repayable on demand	Generally more expensive
Disadvantage	Variable finance cost	Less flexible

250 **B and E**

251 **B**

252 **D**

253 **C**

Section 3

REFERENCES

The Board (2022) *The Conceptual Framework for Financial Reporting*. London: IFRS Foundation

The Board (2022) *IAS 1 Presentation of Financial Reporting*. London: IFRS Foundation.

The Board (2022) *IAS 2 Inventories*. London: IFRS Foundation.

The Board (2022) *IAS 7 Statement of Cash Flows*. London: IFRS Foundation.

The Board (2022) *IAS 10 Events after the Reporting Period*. London: IFRS Foundation.

The Board (2022) *IAS 16 Property, Plant and Equipment*. London: IFRS Foundation.

The Board (2022) *IAS 36 Impairment of Assets*. London: IFRS Foundation.

The Board (2022) *IFRS 5 Non-current Assets Held for Sale and Discontinued Operations*. London: IFRS Foundation.

The Board (2022) *IFRS 16 Leases*